The Greatest Day Ever

The Truth about the Gospel
and the Ten Commandments

Selah Helms & Susan Kahler

BIG BIBLE ANSWERS

The Greatest Day Ever

The Truth about the Gospel
and the Ten Commandments

BOOK 2

Selah Helms & Susan Kahler

CF4•K

10 9 8 7 6 5 4 3 2 1

Copyright © Susan Kahler and Selah Helms

ISBN: 978-1-78191-864-7

epub 978-1-78191-941-5

mobi 978-1-78191-942-2

Published in 2016

by

Christian Focus Publications,

Geanies House, Fearn, Tain,

Ross-shire, IV20 1TW, U.K.

Cover design by Daniel van Straaten

Cover illustration by Jeff Andersen

Other illustrations by Jeff Andersen

Printed and bound by Bell and Bain, Glasgow

Contents

Foreword

As parents, one of our greatest concerns is the spiritual condition of the hearts of our children. Many parents find themselves trusting in "decisions" that their children have made which are actually based on the love of a mythical Jesus, family or peer pressure, emotionalism, the desire for "fire" insurance, an attempt to follow the formula for a good life, or other man-produced motivations. In the end, the true state of the heart is made abundantly clear. True conversion happens as a result of the Holy Spirit using the truth of God to convict, draw, and regenerate the heart.

What parents need most is a deep realization that salvation is a supernatural work of God through the hearing and application of the Word, not a work of us as parents per se. For this reason, the salvation of our children must not be the *goal* of parenting but rather our *desire* given over to the will and purposes of God. What parents need next is to fix their own hearts on the goal of faithfulness to God, for the glory of God. The *chief end* of parenting is to glorify God by doing what He has asked us to do as parents: be faithful to bring to our children His love and care, our changed lives, and above all, His Truth, both taught and practically applied.

This book is a great tool to assist parents in carrying out the faithfulness God asks of us in Deuteronomy 6:7 and Ephesians 6:4. As we were bringing up our children, my wife and I were always looking for resources to help us. I remember teaching through *A Catechism for Boys and Girls,* a basic adaptation of the *Westminster Shorter Catechism.* What a great supplement this work would have been for us!

The last thing we want to do as parents is simply fill our children with information. *Big Bible Answers* is a great tool to encourage personal and practical interaction with God's Word about Himself, the Fall, the Atonement, and our response to His grace. This book is also well organized, creative and beautifully illustrated.

May God bless you as you use this supplemental resource to be faithful in bringing God's Word to your children.

Stuart Scott
Associate Professor of Biblical Counseling
The Southern Baptist Theological Seminary
Louisville, Kentucky

Acknowledgements

The authors wish to thank, first of all, our Lord Jesus Christ for involving us in the spread of His Kingdom on earth, and for giving us truth so worthy of being spread. What a privilege!

Second, we wish to thank our families for their support in making this book a reality — by encouraging us, baby-sitting, and being willing to be independent during the time we spent on the book. We also thank our friends for reading the early drafts to their children and giving us feedback.

Third, we wish to acknowledge certain "trail-blazers" who showed us the importance of doctrine and its practicality for a growing Christian's life: James I. Packer, for his gentle yet powerful way of teaching truth, Jonathan Edwards, for the impact his God-ward thinking had on his own family life for generations, Elizabeth Prentiss, because her tremendous knowledge of God translated into a very practical and active love for others, and C.S. Lewis, who had such a winsome way of capturing children's hearts with deep truth.

May our book in some small measure reflect our reverence for God's truth and our appreciation for the godly influence others have had in our lives!

Introduction

Why Teach Children Doctrine?

It is the authors' hope that this catechism companion will prove a powerful tool with which parents can effectively educate their children in the fundamentals of Christian doctrine.

Christian doctrine is a statement of what the Bible teaches Christians to believe about God and how we can know Him. Orthodox Christian doctrine is based entirely on Holy Scripture. From the time of the Reformation, such doctrine frequently has been taught using some form of catechism, a method of teaching by questions and answers.

However, teaching doctrine is out of fashion with many parents today, even within the church. Instead, some choose to teach character as the basis of their children's spiritual education. Others expect their children to comprehend Christian doctrine strictly by reading Bible stories with them. Some choose an eclectic approach—a little bit of this, a little bit of that, taking the best of several different strands of often conflicting thought and/or approaches. The main goal for them is simply to lead their child in the "sinner's prayer," believing that to be the main hurdle of their child's spiritual experience. Others, wanting their teaching to be practical, purposefully avoid doctrine.

However, it is important to realize that everyone has a doctrine — a way of understanding what the Bible teaches. Everyone who teaches children therefore provides them with some type of doctrine based on the perspective and value judgments he or she brings to life. Thus, we must ensure that the doctrine we teach is sound. All Christian parents want to teach their children biblically. But "biblical" has come to mean a lot of different things to different people. Good, orthodox doctrine arises from a proper understanding of Scripture. Good doctrine provides a grid for being able to plot an understanding of family, daily life, science, history, friendship, emotions, beauty, work, and worship.

Our goal is to equip both parents and children with a robust enough theology to answer the hard questions of life. Good doctrine will direct our thoughts to the right questions: Who is God? What does He require of me? How can I know Him? How can I please Him? Instead, our "felt needs" society directs us to ask how God can solve the little problems of our lives. Our human focus tends to be on how God can fit into our life plans rather than how we fit into His plan. A poor grasp of doctrine, or a wrong doctrine that concentrates on such secondary issues of life, can leave a vacuum in our children's hearts and make them easy prey for any "religious" group that offers them more than they think they are getting. With the question, "why did God make me?" and the answer, "for His own glory, that I might love and obey Him in all

I do," our children can confront all the secondary challenges of life with confidence, peace, and joy. They have the big answer!

Fuzzy doctrine is a natural by-product of a fast-paced society in which most of us tend to be "doers" rather than "thinkers." It is easier. However, those in Christian work often find that, without good reasons for doing so, the people they minister to don't stick with the commitment required to truly take the Christian path. Why? Doing without thinking leads to a flaccid Christianity that struggles to answer the hard questions of life. As Sinclair Ferguson states in *Know Your Christian Life*, the best "thinkers" have historically been the best "doers." The best preachers, martyrs, missionaries, and Christian civic leaders have been those who have grappled with the most challenging biblical teachings.[1] Indeed, the people who have most influenced *us* personally with respect to the gospel are serious students of Bible doctrine, even if they do not consider themselves as such. They are seeking to conform their minds to the Bible's teachings, rather than leading self-serving, busy lives that lack depth.

By-products of good doctrine are righteousness and Christian character. Christian character, as the sole focus and foundation of one's theology, results in nothing but morality. Simultaneously, an absence of strong doctrine naturally leads to looseness in Christian living. (The twenty-first century American church is a showcase for this point.) But teaching that stresses God's holiness and

1. Sinclair B. Ferguson, *Know Your Christian Life* (Downers Grove, IL: InterVarsity Press, 1981), 1.

man's responsibility, along with God's gracious provision of Christ, will produce in individuals a Christian vitality evidenced by love, gratefulness, humility, duty, and service.

Parents who were brought up with "the sinner's prayer" have a challenge on their hands. They may have come to believe that if their children pray that prayer, they are "safe" no matter what they do later in life. Yet a child may pray that prayer without a work of grace truly taking place in his or her heart. Salvation is by grace through faith and not through a particular prayer. The "sinner's prayer" may be, and often is, an expression of faith, but it is not necessarily so. Rather, Scripture teaches that those who believe in Christ become His followers (Luke 9:23), and we must therefore disciple our children over the long haul, teaching them daily and hourly what it means to be followers of Jesus Christ. We must teach them that trust is more than intellectual assent, that those who love Christ will keep His commands (John 14:21), and that we must examine ourselves to see for sure whether our faith is genuine. Leading a child to examine his heart requires time, patience, commitment, and understanding of doctrine, but will be worth far more eternally than giving him or her the false security of a prayer prayed on the surface of his heart.

We have great confidence in the ability of our children to profit from more than a "Bible stories" curriculum and to absorb doctrinal truths from Scripture that will reveal the character of God in a personal way, explain God's provision for us from justification through glorification, and uncover the riches of a salvation that permeates all areas of life.

How To Use This Book

This book is designed to make the discussion and teaching of doctrine pleasant and insightful to children from age 8 and up. Many parents and teachers use a catechism in their instruction of children, yet it can too easily become just an exercise in memorization. The stories and questions in this book will foster open discussion and careful thinking about the ramifications of Bible truths, and the exciting episodes in the lives of real Christians will bring out how these doctrines have shaped history.

The catechism questions (referred to as "Questions to Learn") are grouped into doctrinal points, with a Bible story and a story from subsequent church history to illustrate each section. We suggest that both before and after reading each story in a section, you go over the catechism questions for that section and encourage the children to memorize them. Then tie in the doctrinal concepts with the story events and the Scripture references. We include discussion questions at the end of each story to help accomplish this. Younger children might only learn the catechism questions and enjoy the stories. However, the discussion questions will help older children think through the abstract concepts. Lead the children to see that Bible truths are not separate from our daily lives: they lead us to life! Help them to see that knowing these truths will allow them know the Lord Jesus Christ Himself, and how to rightly worship and please Him.

The catechism that the stories illustrate is taken from *A Catechism for Boys and Girls*, published in the past by Reformation Today Trust. We have slightly edited this helpful work, originally written by Erroll Hulse, to omit some questions on baptism, with the permission of Reformation Today Trust. This children's catechism is an excellent introduction to the *Westminster Shorter Catechism*, *Spurgeon's Baptist Catechism*, and other evangelical Protestant catechisms.

BIBLE STORIES

The Bible stories that we selected to illustrate the catechism's doctrinal truths are imaginatively presented. To some stories we have added dialogue and/or detail that the Scriptures do not give, but in all cases we have sought to retain the accuracy of what the Scriptures do give. The goal is to draw children's imaginations into the biblical accounts, helping them to see the Bible characters as real people in history who were genuinely impacted by doctrinal truths. For those who wish to refer back to the Scriptural accounts, our sources are cited at the end of each story. Note that italicized sentences within the stories are direct quotes from the NIV. All other Scriptures included in the discussion sections are quoted from the ESV.

CHURCH HISTORY

We have made no attempt in this book to comprehensively present church history. Rather, we simply highlight persons and events that give evidence of God's sovereignty and the tremendous impact that doctrine has had on history. Therefore, our primary criterion for choosing the historic stories was their applicability to the biblical truths inherent in the catechism questions. Still, we believe we were able to touch on the most important periods of church history, particularly those that lead up to and explain the sixteenth-century Protestant Reformation.

In choosing between one or more events to illustrate a particular catechism concept, we considered the ages and probable life challenges of our readers. For this reason we tried to minimize the violence. However, Christian history does contain shockingly violent episodes, and we could not disregard the poignant and fitting testimonies of some of the best-known martyrs of the faith.

In addition, wherever possible we have illustrated a doctrinal point with a story of someone championing that truth, rather than failing to live it out. However, in some sections we felt that a negative example was the best teaching tool.

Our church history stories are based on historical facts, though we did add fictional detail (particularly in the dialogue) to make them suitable for elementary age children. None of these additions deviates significantly from any factual information available to us. Bibliographies for each story appear at the end of the book to assist you in providing more historical background when desired. Many of the stories are based primarily on the autobiographical writings of the central characters.

The following story, based on an account from the *Selected Shorter Writings of Benjamin B. Warfield*[2],

2. Benjamin B. Warfield, *Selected Shorter Writings of Benjamin B.*

illustrates how the catechism, taken to heart, can so enlarge a person's thinking as to stir him to godliness even in reactions he himself is unaware of.

No Ordinary Face in the Crowd

The young soldier soberly straightened his uniform and prepared to step off the stagecoach at this, his first post since the Civil War had ended. Surely it would be challenging to keep the peace in this town in the heart of the Confederacy, but he never suspected just how hard it might be.

Before his foot hit the dirt, he heard gunfire, and saw the dust kick up where a bullet had missed its target. Moments later, a lanky gunslinger burst out of a storefront a few feet away, fleeing the shopkeeper's wild bullets. Most of the folk milling boisterously through Main Street dove for cover of whatever kind was available. Many tried to hide behind one another, far more willing for their neighbors to take a stray bullet than they were themselves.

"Take that, you rascal!" the shopkeeper snarled, her skirts flying up all around her. "Don't you ever show your lying, cheating face around here again, or I'll aim a lot closer next time." After she was satisfied that her victim was out of range, she ducked back into her store. The people in the streets emerged crossly, dusted themselves off and quickly scurried for their homes.

It was late in the afternoon and getting toward the hour of day when the bitter, beaten Confederate soldiers had drunk enough to make it dangerous

Warfield–Vol. 1. ed. John E. Meeter (Nutley, NJ: Presbyterian and Reformed Publishing Co., 1970).

for everyone. The speculators and fortune hunters who now controlled all the town's businesses didn't make it any better. They were charging so much for their goods that most regular folks didn't have enough to eat.

The soldier, heading toward his new outpost across town, pitied those in the crowd around him—their faces either pale and drawn, full of fear, or red and puffy, swollen with greed. Amidst this turmoil, he noticed a man approaching him from the opposite end of the street, calmly and purposefully threading his way around a group of quarreling men on one side and an overturned barrel of grain on the other. Confidence, peace, and self-control were etched into this stranger's face. He seemed unruffled by the surrounding chaos, and unafraid.

With much satisfaction, the soldier watched the man while they passed on the street. Unwilling to take his eyes from the serene stranger and return them to the fretful townspeople, the soldier turned to look back at the man's retreating figure. When he did, he found to his surprise that the stranger had also stopped in the street and was looking back at him.

Abruptly, the stranger turned on his heel, came back to the place where the soldier stood staring, and pointed his finger at the brass-buttoned uniform.

"What is the chief end of man?" the stranger demanded.

"To glorify God and enjoy Him forever," came the young man's surprised but spontaneous reply.

"I suspected as much!" the stranger rejoined. "I could tell you were a Shorter Catechism man by the look on your face."

"Why, I thought the same of you," the soldier laughed.

FROM THE BIBLE:

So whether you eat or drink, or whatever you do, do all to the glory of God. (1 Corinthians 10:31)

Bring my sons from afar and my daughters from the ends of the earth, everyone who is called by my name, whom I created for my glory, whom I formed and made. (Isaiah 43:6b-7)

TALKING IT OVER:

1. *Why do you think the stranger asked the soldier the question?*

2. *To glorify something is to give it worship, honor, or to acknowledge its beauty. Do you think these two men glorified God in this situation? Why?*

3. *This young soldier had an unpleasant job to do (glorifying God in a tough situation). Think of something hard that you have to do. How can you give God worship and honor, or acknowledge His beauty in that situation?*

THE FOLLOWING TOPICS AND QUESTIONS
FOLLOW ON FROM BIG BIBLE ANSWERS
VOLUME 1: THE STARRY MESSENGER.

UNIT 4
OUR RESPONSE TO THE GOSPEL

Repentance and Belief

QUESTIONS TO LEARN:

49. **Who will be saved?**
Only those who repent of sin and believe in Christ.

50. **What is it to repent?**
To be sorry for sin, and to hate and forsake it because it is displeasing to God.

51. **What is it to believe in Christ?**
To trust in Christ alone for salvation.

*   *   *

When an earthquake shook the Philippi jail in which Paul and Silas were imprisoned, God used them to bring the frightened Philippian jailer to an earnest trust in Christ. As a teenage boy, the nineteenth-century pastor Charles Spurgeon had long hated and grieved over his youthful sins. After much fruitless searching for relief from this guilt, he was given faith through the simple gospel message – "Look to Christ."

The Earthquake and the Jailer's Broken Heart

On most days the jailer could tolerate his job as the head warden of the Roman prison in Philippi. After all, he had a family to feed, and the pay was good. One could always make more doing a job that no one else wanted to do.

Today had not been such a great one, though. The prison was already overcrowded, and then they had brought him those Christians—Silas and Paul.

As the two severely beaten men were dragged in unconscious, the magistrate had warned the jailer dramatically, "These men are troublemakers; their teaching has provoked rioting throughout the city. Watch them carefully."

Wondering how two such battered men could cause any more trouble, the jailer nevertheless obediently had them taken to the center of the prison and locked into the most secure cell. And, though they were still unconscious, he had their feet shackled, just to be safe. "I hope no one makes me torture them further," he thought.

The jailer decided he had better stick close by since he had been given such strict orders. So he sent the other guards home and settled down for a long night. Soon he was asleep in the outer room.

Some hours later, Paul and Silas awoke and began to sing praises to God. The other prisoners who had seen the pair brought in near death a few hours earlier could not believe their ears. Such melodies had never been heard in these cells before. They listened, quiet and thoughtful.

At midnight, the jail began to tremble. Plaster crumbled from the ceiling in the inner cell, dropping onto Paul and Silas as they began another hymn. Soon, the shaking grew more violent. The prisoners' chains came loose and their prison doors fell open.

The sleeping jailer awoke when he heard iron clanging against iron. Disoriented, he wondered where he was. Then came the horrible moment when he saw that the cell doors stood wide open and he recalled how heavily the prisoners outnumbered him. If they had not already escaped through the back door, they could easily overpower him now.

"This will cost me my life," he thought. The rule for operating prisons was a simple one: if a criminal escaped, the careless jailer responsible for it would pay for the crime in his place.

"But," the fearful jailer thought, "I will not put my family through a disgraceful trial. I will carry out the sentence on myself." Pulling the sword from his belt, he pointed it at his own chest and was just about to thrust when a shout came from within the inner cell.

"Don't harm yourself! We are all here," Paul called out. Thinking himself delirious, the jailer lit a lamp, looked in, and found that his prisoners

were indeed all still there, though not one of them remained chained.

He fell trembling at Paul and Silas' feet, his shocked mind vividly recounting all the things he had heard about these men and their master, Jesus Christ. They said Jesus was the Son of God and forgave sins. Should he have listened more closely to their message? Instead he had unwittingly taken part in a Roman quarrel against God. How could he have helped to persecute them so, shackling them when they were too weak to stand up? Yet here they stood, beaming at him amidst the rubble of a jail that could no longer hold them!

In the face of Silas and Paul's joy and faith, the jailer was acutely aware of an eternal need in his soul. He thought about how long he had pursued his own selfish course. Where was it leading him? Though he now saw what a sudden, certain thing death was, the jailer had never before considered what lay beyond it. He asked desperately, *"Sirs, what must I do to be saved?"*

"Believe in the Lord Jesus, and you will be saved, my friend,* Paul answered him. And the Philippian jailer did believe.

Then he took Paul and Silas back to his own house, washed their wounds, and woke his household. They listened to Paul explain the whole truth about Jesus, and every one of them repented and believed in Him. That very night, Paul and Silas baptized them.

At daybreak, the rejoicing jailer received an unexpected order from the magistrate to release the apostles. "Why, it is almost as if they were sent to my jail just for me," he thought joyfully. "Imagine all the suffering on my behalf. How much God has loved me, even while I ignored my sin and persecuted my Savior!"

(Taken from Acts 16:16-36)

FROM THE BIBLE:

"For God so loved the world, that he gave his only Son, that whoever believes in him should not perish but have eternal life. For God did not send his Son into the world to condemn the world, but in order that the world might be saved through him." (John 3:16-17)

Or do you presume on the riches of his kindness and forbearance and patience, not knowing that God's kindness is meant to lead you to repentance? (Romans 2:4)

TALKING IT OVER:

1. *One way God leads us to repent of our sins is to show us His holiness and power so that we can see how sinful and weak we are in comparison to him. How did God show the jailer his holiness and power? How did the jailer feel about God and Himself as a result?*

2. *Another way God leads us to repent is to show us His mercy and love so that we turn away from our sin and seek to please Him. How did God show the jailer His mercy and love?*

3. *When the Philippian jailer asked Paul and Silas how he could be saved, what one thing did they tell him?*

4. *Can we be saved from our sins by believing in anything else but Jesus, or by doing anything else besides believe in Him? Why not?*

"Look Unto *Me*"

Fifteen-year-old Charles Haddon Spurgeon descended the back stairs at the Newmarket school where he was both pupil and underteacher for the younger students. He tried to put something of a spring in his step so that anyone he might meet up with besides old Mary the cook would not see his misery. When he entered the kitchen, Charles found Mary alone in the pantry sorting potatoes.

At once Mary detected the boy's torment. She had seen it on his face before, and had lately spent much time on her knees on his behalf. "Charlie, sit yourself down and tell me your trouble, son," she commanded, snatching a stool out of nowhere and plopping it down next to a large pile of potatoes.

With a heavy sigh, Charles sat down. When he thought he could speak without crying, he told her, "Mary, I ... I, I'm afraid God is going to send me to hell!" There, he'd said it, but didn't seem to feel any better having done so.

"All right, Charlie. What makes you think so?" she asked, patting his arm.

"Because I can't stop, I just can't stop sinning, Mary, no matter how I promise to and set my mind against all the things I know God hates.

Why, I can't even make myself tell you what I was thinking just last night. It took me until this morning to stop thinking those thoughts, and still they are just under the surface ready to rise up in my mind again. I can feel it, Mary. I won't be able to keep them out for long.

"Don't you see what this means? God wouldn't be righteous if He would tolerate such things from me! And I know He won't, Mary. God *is* righteous, and He is just. He *should* send me to hell. But I can't bear it. What am I going to do?"

"Charlie, I can tell you that the way to God for all of us is Jesus Christ. He's the one who paid for your sins, and he's coming for you, son. I believe that. I've been asking God for that, and you need to as well. Now go. I must have breakfast on the table shortly!"

When Charles went home to Colchester for Christmas break a few days later, he still didn't really understand what Mary had told him. He had certainly been asking God for mercy, but he simply couldn't believe that a just God would forgive the wretchedness he saw in his own heart. He could think of nothing that he could possibly do to persuade God to forgive him for all this!

Each Sunday during the break, Charles roused himself out of the despair that threatened to overwhelm him, and went to church hoping that in one of the sermons he would hear what his heart so longed to know—what did he need to do to have his sins forgiven? But each Sunday he was disappointed by sermons that seemed to answer every question but the one he asked.

On Sunday, January 6th, 1850, Charles awoke while it was still dark. Outside, snow fell heavily onto Colcester and the surrounding countryside. Inside, his heart fell further into hopeless sorrow even as he searched his Bible and prayed for the answer to his question.

Later that morning, Charles set out for a church his parents had told him about. But God had a different plan. A snowdrift blocked his path and diverted him into another church — a tiny Primitive Methodist chapel down a nearby side street. Only a dozen or so others had made it through the storm that morning, but the preacher was not among

them. As Charles joined the small group, a very simple-looking fellow, probably a shoemaker or tailor, slid out of his pew and stepped up to the pulpit.

"The text this mornin' is 'Look unto me, and be ye saved.' Isaiah 45:22," he managed to stammer out, barely able to read. "My dear friends, this is a very simple text. It says, 'Look.' You see, *anybody* can look. You don't need a college education to look. It's not hard work. You don't have to lift your hand or even your finger to look. Why, a fool can do it. A child can do it. A poor man or a rich one. Just 'look.'

"But look at what? It says here, 'Look unto *me*.' That is Christ. Don't look to yourself and say, 'What can *I* do?' but look unto *Christ*. Don't look to God the Father and say, 'Am I one of your chosen ones?' Just look at *Christ*. Jesus says, 'Look unto me; I'm hanging on a cross for you, sweatin' great drops of blood. Look unto me; I'm dead and buried, and rise again, for you. Look unto *me*, where I've risen to sit at the Father's right hand and plead for Him to see you through my blood. Oh sinner, look unto *me*.'"

About that time, the tailor pointed at Charles and said, "Young man, you seem altogether miserable. And you always will be until you obey this text. You have nothin' to do but look. Look at Jesus Christ and live."[1]

Charles heard nothing else the man said. His eyes left his own dejected self, and found Jesus in all his glory. "Of course," he thought, "here is God's mercy, his forgiveness, and his justice. This is the way to salvation. It's not me; it's all in Him."

When Charles returned home, his family saw that the cloud had been lifted. "Tell us what wonderful thing has happened to you," his mother encouraged.

Charles Spurgeon never stopped telling the people of England about the marvelous Savior

---

1. Spurgeon's recollections of this sermon are quoted more fully in: Ernest W. Bacon, *Spurgeon: Heir of the Puritans*, (London: George Allen & Unwin, 1967), 23-24 (from a March 1861 sermon of Spurgeon); and Hugh T. Kerr and John M. Mulder, eds., *Famous Conversions, the Christian Experience* (Grand Rapids: Wm. B. Eerdmans Publishing Co., 1983), 129-132 (from *The Autobiography of Charles H. Spurgeon*).

who cleanses us from our wretched sin when we look at Him and believe. Spurgeon became one of the most influential ministers of the nineteenth century, respected for his passionate faithfulness to God's Word in an age when many others had grown complacent and worldly in their attitudes toward the Lord.

FROM THE BIBLE:

As it is, I rejoice, not because you were grieved, but because you were grieved into repenting. . . . For godly grief produces a repentance that leads to salvation without regret, whereas worldly grief produces death. (2 Corinthians 7:9a, 10)

And the Lord said to Moses, "Make a fiery serpent and set it on a pole, and everyone who is bitten, when he sees it, shall live." (Numbers 21:8)

"And as Moses lifted up the serpent in the wilderness, so must the Son of Man be lifted up, that whoever believes in him may have eternal life. (John 3:14-15)

TALKING IT OVER:

1. *From the story, how do you know that Charles Spurgeon repented of his sins?*

2. *Repentance alone is not enough to be saved from our sin. What else is needed?*

3. *How did God lead Charles Spurgeon to believe in Jesus Christ for his salvation?*

The Holy Spirit

Questions to learn:

52. **Can you repent and believe in Christ by your own power?**
No. I can do nothing good without God's Holy Spirit.

53. **How can you receive the Holy Spirit?**
God has told us that we must pray to Him for the Holy Spirit.

*　　　　*　　　　*

God's Holy Spirit enables us to repent and believe. The Holy Spirit led Paul to Philippi to proclaim the truth about Christ to Lydia and her household, and thereafter opened Lydia's heart to understand her need for a Savior. Over the years, however, many overzealous preachers have not trusted in God's Spirit to accomplish a genuine, inward work of grace in people's lives. One such man was the famous nineteenth-century revivalist Charles Finney, whose preaching often worked people into an emotional fervor that they sadly mistook for salvation.

The Opened Heart

Claudius admired the selection of sheer linens that his supplier had spread across the floor of his gift stall in the Philippi marketplace. "Lydia, you must have every color imaginable, but my favorite is still the 'royal purple.' And it's my best seller too. The wealthy Roman officials are especially fond of it."

Lydia accepted Claudius' compliment with a smile. She imported the "royal purple" from her business contacts back in Thyatira, and had already noticed how much it was in demand among the Roman soldiers and dignitaries who were now living in Philippi. She had certainly made her move to this bustling town at just the right moment, financially speaking.

But money had not really been her motive. She still was not quite sure why she had decided to uproot her household and move to a new province. After all, it was especially hard for her to practice her religion here, since there were so few Jews in Philippi. They didn't even have a synagogue in which to meet. She herself was not a Jew, but she had come to see that the God of the Jewish Scriptures was the only true God. Somehow she felt that He had drawn her here, that He was trying to show her something she had been unable to see before.

Ten miles east, in the coastal town of Neapolis, Paul was getting off the ship from Troas. He and his companions—Silas, Luke and Timothy—were on a mission trip from Antioch.

Before sailing, the group had tried to go into two other provinces, but the Holy Spirit had shut the door on those attempts. Then Paul had had a dream about a man from Macedonia, the province that included Philippi. In the dream the

man had begged Paul to come there and help the Macedonians. So Paul and his companions had traveled from Troas to Neapolis, and the door was open wide. They had only to seek out those whose hearts the Holy Spirit was opening to Christ.

The missionaries made their way first to Philippi, arriving just before the Sabbath. Early in the morning of their day of worship, they left the city through the west gate and made their way to the Gangites River, where they had planned to find a quiet place to pray.

Lydia, too, headed toward the river at the first signs of dawn. She had all the women of her household in tow—the personal servants, the weavers, those who cleaned and dyed the fabrics. They would join the group of God-fearing worshipers at the Gangites.

The women were already in prayer at the riverbank when Paul's group arrived. Seeing them, Paul urgently felt their need for Jesus.

"Have any of you heard about Jesus of Nazareth, the one who was crucified in Jerusalem and on the third day was resurrected to eternal life?" he began.

At the mention of the name, Lydia's heart beat a little faster. "We heard talk of Him before we moved here from Thyatira," she conceded. "Who was he?"

"He is the one who sent me to you," Paul said. "His Holy Spirit led me to come to Macedonia and find those whose hearts the Lord was preparing to receive salvation. Before He was crucified, Jesus promised to send His Spirit to reveal the truth about Himself to His chosen people who would recognize Him as their Savior."

As Paul spoke, that same Spirit of God opened Lydia's heart to all that Paul said so that she understood and joyfully embraced the good news about Christ. This was what she had been yearning for. The women of her household also believed, and all were baptized there on the banks of the Gangites by the four missionaries.

From that moment on, Lydia supported Paul's Macedonian ministry in whatever ways she could. She no longer considered herself her own, but put her home and wealth at God's disposal with great thankfulness for the work He had done in her heart.

(Taken from Acts 16:6-15)

FROM THE BIBLE:

One who heard us was a woman named Lydia, from the city of Thyatira, a seller of purple goods, who was a worshiper of God. The Lord opened her heart to pay attention to what was said by Paul. (Acts 16:14)

If you then, who are evil, know how to give good gifts to your children, how much more will the heavenly Father give the Holy Spirit to those who ask him! (Luke 11:13)

TALKING IT OVER:

1. Who was responsible for Lydia's belief in Jesus Christ as her Savior?

2. What were some of the many ways that the Holy Spirit acted in her life and Paul's to bring this about?

3. Was it only for Lydia that the Holy Spirit gave her the gift of faith? After God gives us faith, how might he use us to encourage faith in others?

The Man Who Tried to Save Evans Mills

On an evening late in the spring of 1824, a sizable crowd filled the schoolhouse in Evans Mills, New York. Tonight Charles Grandison Finney would light a revivalist fire that would blaze across the American frontier.

But that night, Finney was not happy with what went on. As he warmed to his preaching — explaining yet again about God's judgment and about salvation through Christ — Finney observed his audience. One man in the third row was dozing while his wife smiled and nodded her head now and then at what Finney said. The others also looked pleased with his sermon, when they weren't whispering back and forth making plans for Sunday dinner.

"Why, I've been preaching to them every night for weeks, and they are still staring at me with the same glazed-over serenity. They just don't get it," Finney thought. "I believe it's time to light a fire under their carefree hides."

He stopped mid-sentence and glared at his congregation for a long moment. The woman in the third row nudged her husband awake. Then Finney shouted loudly, "Do you admit that what I've been preaching is the truth? Well, *do* you?"

Rows of sinners gazed back at him, speechless.

"Most or all of you profess to believe it. But do you really? Know that if you do not repent and believe this moment, then you are rejecting the Lord's gospel. Who is ready to do what he ought to do? A horse may trample you to death tonight and you may never get another chance. Now what will it be?" He raised his voice even louder, and reached far over the lectern pointing his finger around the room. "Those of you who are ready right now to commit to God, stand up. Those of you who are not interested in salvation, just sit there."

For what seemed like many minutes, not a head was turned or a breath exhaled. But all eyes discreetly flitted around the room to see what the others would do. No one moved an inch.

"Very well," Finney declared, "you have made your choice! You have rejected the Savior. Now go home. I will only preach one more night here, and then I'll move on to a town where people are willing to turn from their sins and follow Christ. I just hope you are all able to come back here tomorrow night." Then Finney watched silently as the congregation, stunned and bewildered, filed out of the schoolhouse.

The next night, Finney tells us in his memoirs, the anxious townspeople followed him through the streets and packed the schoolhouse "to its utmost capacity." Would this really be their last chance to repent? Who would do it? No one wanted to miss out on the hubbub. Some didn't want to miss out on salvation. Almost everyone was there.

That night, Finney told the people of Evans Mills everything he knew about hell. He preached for more than an hour, describing in great detail the misery of eternity apart from God. By the end of his sermon, the children were weeping into their mothers' laps, all the men were pale, and some of the women had fainted away at the prospect of what lay before them. Just as Finney had planned, the congregation was now a powder keg of emotions.

Finney looked down on them fiercely. "I'll be right here tomorrow night," he said, and again abruptly walked out of the schoolhouse. He had given them no chance to repent! The stage was set.

Over the next several nights, the people poured into the schoolhouse in a state of high agitation. Those of every religious and moral persuasion squeezed in. One man brought his gun and threatened to kill Finney for working his wife up into a terrified fervor. Finney took no notice, but preached his heart out and commanded them, "Now, sinners, do your duty and repent of your transgressions. It will be told tonight in heaven and hell what you decide to do. Here is the window you can jump through to salvation. It's open just a bit. Come to the front right now if you choose the way of Christ!"

Revival had come to Evans Mills. Or so it seemed.

As Finney honed his revival style, the people of Evans Mills and nearby towns in which he preached were powerfully moved. On many nights, as he threatened and shamed them, dozens leapt up and made their way to the front. Some came groaning and yelling. Some got only a few steps before they fell to the ground weeping or bawling. Others joined the fray not wanting to be left behind, struggling to the front just to see what would happen. In the end, Finney was quite satisfied that the people in and around Evans Mills had come to their senses and grabbed hold of salvation.

Although few doubted that Charles Finney knew the Lord Himself, many in his day and since have condemned his methods. He preached as if people could repent of their sins and believe in Christ in their own power, simply by deciding to. It was true that some genuinely came to Christ during these services, but many who thought they had been converted during Finney's revival meetings had only had their feelings stirred up. Lacking the Holy Spirit's conviction, they were not truly sorry for their sins and did not really trust in Christ. They went forward only because their emotions were inflamed—they feared hell, or they thought they wouldn't get another chance. Some went forward just because everyone else did. Sadly, some of them never recovered from the confusion and disappointment of their "revival" experiences.

FROM THE BIBLE:

Now we have received not the spirit of the world, but the Spirit who is from God, that we might understand the things freely given us by God. (1 Corinthians 2:12)

"Not everyone who says to me, 'Lord, Lord,' will enter the kingdom of heaven, but the one who does the will of my Father who is in heaven. On that day many will say to me, 'Lord, Lord, did we not prophesy in your name, and cast out demons in your name, and do many mighty works in your name?' And then will I declare to them, 'I never knew you; depart from me, you workers of lawlessness.'" (Matthew 7:21-23)

TALKING IT OVER:

1. *Remember that repentance means being sorry for sin and forsaking it because it displeases God. Do you think all of the people who came forward in Charles Finney's revival in Evans Mills really became Christians? Why?*

2. *What does God give us to help us repent of sin and believe in Christ for forgiveness? Can we repent and believe without the Holy Spirit's help?*

3. *Do you think there are people who appear to believe in Christ when they really don't? How do you know if you are truly a Christian? (A true Christian will want to do God's will, and will have some evidence of the Holy Spirit in his life. See Matthew 7 above).*

Those Before Christ

Questions to learn:

54. How were godly persons saved before the coming of Christ?

By believing in the Savior to come.

55. How did they show their faith?

By offering sacrifices on God's altar.

56. What did these sacrifices represent?

Christ, the Lamb of God, who was to die for sinners.

*   *   *

After God had allowed the Jews to be exiled in Babylon for many years, he brought a remnant back to Judea to reconstruct his temple and reinstitute the sacrifices that the Law required. Obedient Jews such as Zerubbabel, who led the remnant back, surely longed for the Messiah whom God's prophets had promised would redeem them from their sins once and for all. Centuries later, the Maccabees reclaimed the temple from Greek invaders who had desecrated it. Their zeal for the sacrificial system was rooted in their faith that God would forgive their sins.

The Greatest Day Ever

The streets surrounding Jerusalem's glistening new temple were crowded with Jewish people who had returned from the Babylonian exile. They and their families were joined by many non-Jewish Persians — curiosity seekers who wondered what all the commotion was about. Zerubbabel, the Jewish leader who was a descendant of King David, strolled among the merrymakers enjoying the greatest day of his life.

As he dodged a group of musicians dancing across the temple yard, Zerubbabel remembered back to when this adventure had begun — twenty-three years ago when the Lord had moved the heart of King Cyrus to send some of the exiled Jews home to rebuild Solomon's temple. Zerubbabel, a strapping young man then, had awakened one morning to find that God had given him a passion to lead the returning remnant.

The first great day of Zerubbabel's life was the day they had arrived in Jerusalem — all 50,000 of them with their livestock and household goods, as well as with the sacred temple furnishings that Nebuchadnezzar had stolen when he had destroyed the temple a generation before. Later that year, they had completed the rebuilding of the temple altar and made the first animal sacrifices to the Lord since the Babylonians had taken them captive years ago. How grateful Zerubbabel had been for the opportunity to once again obey God's command to shed the blood of unblemished animals in atonement for the people's many grievous violations of his laws!

Not long after that, he and Jeshua, the high priest, had directed the people to lay the foundation for the new temple. The Lord had blessed this work, and they had held a huge celebration on the day of

its completion. Zerubbabel, waving at old Jeshua on the presentation platform now, remembered how the priest had paraded across the temple foundation dressed in his bright vestments, blasting a trumpet in praise to God. Oh, how the people had shouted and sung to the Lord on that day!

Following this celebration, however, the good days had been rarer. The Persians, who were afraid of the Jewish God, had begun to harass Zerubbabel, Jeshua and the temple workers. And the Jews, rather than trusting God to provide a way for them to do what he had commanded, had given up building the temple and instead set to work enlarging their own homes and planting their fields. The foundation of the Lord's temple had lain bare for sixteen bleak years.

One day, a voice had roused the people from their apathy, shouting: "'Leave your plush homes and build my house, *so that I may take pleasure in it and be honored,*' commands the Lord your God." The voice was that of God's prophet Haggai. When they heard it, Zerubbabel and the people had repented of their fear and selfishness, and began to build. Through Haggai, and his fellow prophet Zechariah, God had encouraged them all along the way: "'*Be strong, oh Zerubbabel. Be strong, oh Jeshua.* Be strong, all you my people, *and work. For I am with you,*' declares the Lord. '*My Spirit remains among you. Do not fear.*'"

And the Lord's Spirit had guided them and protected their work on his house. Zerubbabel had especially relished the day that their pagan governor had written to the new Persian king, Darius, whining about their progress on the temple. Darius, though, wrote back ordering the governor not to interfere with the rebuilding, but instead to pay the building expenses out of the royal treasury!

Today, towering before Zerubbabel, was their finished work. He had lived to see God fulfill his promises to them. In his joy, Zerubbabel leapt onto the presentation platform and quieted the people. He raised his hands and prayed, "Oh, righteous and almighty God, who delivered our forefathers out of captivity, who disciplined our fathers by sending them into exile, and who has blessed this remnant of your people, we praise your name. Here is your house—the house you have allowed us to build for you! May it honor you always.

"Lord, we look forward to an even greater day than this—the coming of our Messiah whom your prophet Zechariah has told us will one day rise up out of the house of David as a fountain that will cleanse us from our sin and impurity. But today, oh Lord, we offer the blood of these animals in accordance with your command to Moses."

Zerubbabel nodded to Jeshua then, who went forward to the altar of the Lord and sacrificed twelve unblemished goats, one for the sins of each of the tribes of Israel.

(Taken from Ezra 1:1–6:18; Haggai 1:1-2:9; Zechariah 12:10-13:1)

From the Bible:

For since the law has but a shadow of the good things to come instead of the true form of these realities, it can never, by the same sacrifices that are continually offered every year, make perfect those who draw near... Consequently, when Christ came into the world, he said, "Sacrifices and offerings you have not desired, but a body have you prepared for me; in burnt offerings and sin offerings you have taken no pleasure. Then I said, 'Behold, I have come to do your will, O God, as it is written of me in the scroll of the book.'" ... And by that will we have been sanctified through the offering of the body of Jesus Christ once for all. (Hebrews 10:1, 5-7, 10)

Talking it Over:

1. *Why was it so important for the Jews to rebuild the temple and reinstitute the sacrifices for their sins? (Because God had commanded them to make such sacrifices. See Leviticus 4. Without the shedding of blood, there could be no forgiveness of sins. See Hebrews 9:22.)*

2. *Although the remnant of Jews who returned to Jerusalem was obedient to God's command to sacrifice animals, did they rely on these sacrifices to secure God's forgiveness? On whom did they actually rely for God's forgiveness? How did they know about the coming Messiah who would purify them once and for all eternity?*

3. *Why do we not sacrifice animals to atone for our sins today?*

The Maccabees: Defenders of God's Altar

Benjamin ducked behind a boulder about twenty feet from the fork in the road that led north and west out of Jerusalem. He was sure he had felt the vibration of approaching horses. No doubt these were King Antiochus' men hunting down Jews who had escaped Jerusalem over the last few gruesome months. Benjamin tucked his legs up tight, trying to disappear within a crag in the rocks. He clutched the letter he was to deliver to Mattathias, priest of the village of Modein. He had been instructed to swallow it if he was in danger of being captured.

The pounding hoofs came, thundered close, and then receded toward the north. They had not taken the road to Modein! There was still time. Benjamin crawled out and ran toward the setting sun.

Mattathias and his five grown sons had just finished dinner when they heard a knock at the door. The sons watched Mattathias nervously as he rose to answer it. These days even the most routine occurrences seemed threatening.

Mattathias found Benjamin outside, hurried him in, and took the letter. Anxiously, he sat down at the table and began to read while his sons waited.

When Mattathias finally raised his head, his face was a fierce red, and tears spilled out of his flaming eyes. "My sons …" was all he managed to say. One of them — Judas, also known as Maccabeus — gently took the note from his father's shaking hand and read aloud:

> My dear old friend Mattathias, I write to warn you that the unthinkable has happened. After killing every Jew in Jerusalem who refused to violate God's laws in one of the many contemptible ways that our Greek "king" could devise, his men invaded and pillaged the sacred temple itself, violating even the most Holy of Holies. As their crowning dishonor to our Lord, they erected a statue of the pagan god Zeus above the temple altar, and then sacrificed a pig to this vulgar image. Of course, they chose a pig because they know that under God's law this animal is unclean.
>
> As you might imagine, the devout among us have fled the city in hopes of avoiding the horrible choice that Antiochus has given us: disobey our God or be slaughtered like sheep. But his men are intent on hunting us down, so the choice remains. Soon you must make it too, as Antiochus is extending his brutality into the outlying villages. Mattathias, it is only a matter of time before they arrive in Modein. Be prepared to die well, my friend.

Judas let the letter fall to the floor and grabbed both of his father's arms. "There is a way we can die well that your friend has not thought of, Father," he said, staring steadily into the older man's sorrowful eyes.

Mattathias understood, and found strength in his son's words. There was indeed a third alternative, and they would take it: they would die defending their holy altar.

Early one morning a few days later, an official named Apelles led a detachment of the king's troops into Modein. Apelles positioned the heavily armed men around the village, and set a few to work building an altar to Zeus. They had brought along a pig.

When all was ready for the pagan sacrifice, the soldiers paraded the villagers into the square to watch. Because they were the priestly family of the village, Mattathias and his sons were forced to lead the procession.

When all were in place, Apelles clutched the hilt of his sword menacingly and approached Mattathias. "You are the leader here," Apelles said so that all could hear. "Be the first in Modein to carry out the king's order. Sacrifice this animal to Zeus and receive abundant favors from the throne." With that, he waved his free hand toward the pig standing on the new altar, inviting Mattathias to approach.

Mattathias said nothing for a long while as he calmly fingered the sacrificial knife in his hand and glared at Apelles. The village was deathly quiet. Accepting Apelles' offer would be a clear violation of God's law and would make a mockery of the sacrificial system that God had ordained since the time of Moses. Finally Mattathias announced: "I and my sons will follow the Lord's covenant though all others may tremble and fall before the king. We will not deviate one step from God's Law."

Preparing for the worst, the villagers hid their children's eyes. But just as Apelles drew his sword to take off Mattathias' head, an ambitious young man from the crowd stepped onto the pagan altar. "I will accept the king's favors," he said eagerly.

Relieved, Apelles and his men helped prepare the pig for slaughter. When all was ready, the young man drew his arm back to slice into the animal. At this moment of sacrilege, outrage consumed Mattathias, and he rushed forward to stab the traitor with his own sacrificial knife. Before they could subdue the pious priest and the other villagers, Apelles and his men had also perished. The pagan altar quickly followed.

Mattathias then called out to his brethren, "Whoever is zealous for God's Law and will pledge himself to maintain God's covenant with his people, follow me and my sons!" The Maccabean revolt had begun.

When the Jewish refugees hiding throughout the Judean countryside heard of the events in Modein, they rallied behind the Maccabees, choosing to die fighting for God's Law. Eventually, they succeeded in regaining the temple that Zerubbabel and his brethren had constructed 350 years before, and they reinstituted the sacrifices that the Lord had commanded them to make in atonement for their sins.

It would not be long now before Jesus, the perfect and eternal sacrifice for our sins, would come to earth and live among the Jews of Judea. The shedding of *His* blood would forever atone for the sins of those who had or would repent and believe in Him.

FROM THE BIBLE:

Then [Moses] took the Book of the Covenant and read it in the hearing of the people. And they said, "All that the Lord has spoken we will do, and we will be obedient." And Moses took the blood and threw it on the people and said, "Behold the blood of the covenant that the Lord has made with you in accordance with all these words." (Exodus 24:7-8)

But when Christ appeared as a high priest of the good things that have come, then through the greater and more perfect tent (not made with hands, that is, not of this creation) he entered once for all into the holy place, not by means of the blood of goats and calves but by means of his own blood, thus securing an eternal redemption. ...Therefore he is the mediator of a new covenant, so that those who are called may receive the promised eternal inheritance, since a death has occurred that redeems them from the transgressions committed under the first covenant. (Hebrews 9:11-12, 15)

TALKING IT OVER:

1. *Why was Mattathias so upset that the temple built by Zerubbabel was used to make sacrifices to Zeus?*

2. *Why was the sacrificial system so important to the Jews? (The Law required it; it was tied to their worship of God and their hope of His forgiveness of their sins.)*

3. *The Jews who lived before Christ were under the "first covenant" that is discussed in the above verses. Look again at Hebrews 9:15. Whose blood atoned for the sins of those who were under this first covenant?*

Jesus is Prophet, Priest, King

QUESTIONS TO LEARN:

57. What does Christ do for his people?

He does the work of a prophet, a priest, and a king.

58. Why is Christ a prophet?

Because he teaches us the will of God.

59. Why is Christ a priest?

Because he died for our sins and prays to God for us.

60. Why is Christ a king?

Because he rules over us and defends us.

61. Why do you need Christ as a prophet?

Because I am ignorant.

62. Why do you need Christ as a priest?

Because I am guilty.

63. Why do you need Christ as a king?

Because I am weak and helpless.

*   *   *

Through Jesus' response to Peter's sad blunders, Peter grew to love the Lord Jesus deeply as his prophet, priest and king. Two who powerfully experienced Christ's kingship were Adoniram and Ann Judson, America's first foreign missionaries.

If Christ Is for Us, Who Can Be Against Us?

The main road through Jerusalem was not rugged, yet Peter stumbled along it like a man who had already walked a long way through rough terrain. He and John were trying to keep pace with the detachment of soldiers that had bound Jesus before the disciples' very eyes, and were now hurrying Him through the city. They could just see the soldiers' torches and spears above the heads of the Jewish festival-goers crowding the street.

Peter searched his mind for something he could hang onto—a safe thought. What he found instead were many frightening things to avoid. So much had happened in such a short time! During their Passover meal, just that evening, Jesus had washed the disciples' feet and had spoken a great deal about pouring out his blood. If that weren't bad enough, Jesus then announced that one of the Twelve would betray Him, and that they would all fall away from Him on that very evening.

After that, things had happened quickly. Not wanting to fall away from their Lord as he had warned, the disciples had followed Jesus to the garden at Gethsemane—all except Judas, who had soon appeared in the garden leading several Jewish officials and the soldiers who seized Jesus. Peter himself had pulled his sword and swung wildly at the nearest intruder, cutting off his ear. Remembering this as he staggered along the path, Peter gazed at his guilty hands. Had he really done that?

Then there was something else Jesus had said to Peter before the soldiers had come. What was it? Peter chased the memory around his mind but it would not be caught. It seemed important, but Peter simply wasn't in any shape to supervise his poor rattled brain. It would have to wait.

John and Peter soon arrived at the gate of Annas, the former high priest, into whose home Jesus had been taken. John knew him well and convinced the guard at the door to let him inside. Peter, it was decided, would have to wait in the courtyard with the other onlookers.

The servant who opened the courtyard gate to Peter eyed him suspiciously. He was not in soldier's uniform, and she didn't recognize him as one of the Jewish officials who so often came around. "Aren't you one of *his* disciples?" she asked him accusingly.

Peter cringed at the way she said "his"—with hatred and disgust. Beyond her in the courtyard he could see men warming themselves over a fire. Some of them were probably close enough to overhear. Why should he have to answer to a servant anyway?

"I am not," he lied, and moved quickly past her to the fire.

The men already sitting around it were chatting breathlessly about the evening's events. Most of them had families at home waiting on them to celebrate the Passover, but none wanted to be left out of the excitement. No, they would all wait and see what would be done with Jesus.

"My bet is they let him go," said an older man who had been around long enough to watch plenty of blasphemers fall in and out of favor.

"Not a chance," argued the young aide of an official who was inside. "Why, He's a menace. He's got hundreds believing His lies, and ... He stirs people up. One of His men tried to kill the high priest's servant this very evening!"

Had the fire not already chafed Peter's face, the others would have seen it turn red at this reference to his impetuous swordplay in the garden.

Just then, a third man noticed Peter's clothing. "Say, aren't you one of the Galileans who travels with Him?" he asked.

Peter's eyes darted from one penetrating gaze to another within the tight circle of blazing faces. *"Man, I am not!"* Peter denied.

A minor official who had overheard these remarks then stepped into the circle. "Yes," he said, pointing at Peter, "didn't I see you with Him earlier in the olive grove?"

Exasperated by their needling accusations, and fearful for his own life, Peter retorted now in a loud voice, *"Man, I don't know what you are talking about!"* Before anyone could respond to this, however, a fitful rooster crowed from the high priest's yard. As Peter instinctively turned toward the sound, he saw Jesus watching him sorrowfully from the doorway of Annas' house.

The memory that Peter had been unable to grasp earlier now rushed in and claimed his whole attention. Jesus had said to him: "Peter, Peter, Satan has asked to have you. But I have prayed for you, that your faith will not fail. Before the rooster crows tonight, you will claim three times not to know me. *But when you have turned back, strengthen your brothers."*

Peter tore his eyes from his Savior, ran from the courtyard, and wept bitterly.

(Taken from Luke 22:31-34, 54-62; John 18:10-27)

From the Bible:

My little children, I am writing these things to you so that you may not sin. But if anyone does sin, we have an advocate with the Father, Jesus Christ the righteous. He is the propitiation for our sins, and not for ours only but also for the sins of the whole world. (1 John 2:1-2)

For we do not have a high priest who is unable to sympathize with our weaknesses, but one who in every respect has been tempted as we are, yet without sin. (Hebrews 4:15)

Talking it Over:

1. *How was Christ a prophet in this story? (He knew beforehand what would happen, warned Peter of it, and knew what to do about it.)*

2. *How was Christ a priest in this story? (He interceded to God on Peter's behalf, then offered the sacrifice of himself.)*

3. *How would it make you feel if you knew that the Lord Jesus Christ was praying to the Father on your behalf?*

King Over All Kings

Adoniram Judson and James Colman bowed low to the floor while awaiting the appearance of the Burman king, referred to by all as the Golden Presence. When young King Bagyidaw finally strutted into the audience hall, Adoniram stole a look. With his long black hair wound up in a turban, the Golden Presence was small but regal, wearing checkered silk pants and carrying a gold-sheathed sword.

At length, the king acknowledged the two American missionaries who knelt before him, and beckoned to the official standing by with a petition that Adoniram had written on palm leaves. The missionaries had come several days' journey upriver from Rangoon in hopes that the king's Golden Ears would hear their plea. "Very well," the king said to the official, "read."

The petition respectfully begged that the king issue an order stating that any of his Burman subjects who desired to practice the Christian religion should be allowed to do so in peace. The king pondered this for a moment, and then took his hand from the hilt of his sword and snatched the palm leaf from the cowering official. Adoniram also handed the king a carefully worded, palm leaf-sized statement of his Christian beliefs.

While the king read the two documents, Adoniram prayed fervently for God to soften this cruel man's heart so that he would allow the gospel of Jesus to be shared openly in Burma. Adoniram remembered the day, seven years ago, when he and his wife Ann had arrived in this godless country as the first American missionaries abroad. He thought of her now, waiting for him at their mission in Rangoon, trying to protect the three timid but sincere Burmans who had only recently come to believe in Christ. These converts had faced threats so severe, that before he had left for the palace in Ava, two of them had asked to be baptized at night so as not to advertise their new status as Christians. All that could change, though, if King Bagyidaw would only grant his people permission to worship as God led them.

The Golden Presence read no further than Adoniram's claim that there is only one true God. At that point he looked up darkly and opened his hand, allowing the palm leaves to flutter to the floor. The interview was over, the petition denied. Adoniram and James Colman were instantly cast out of the palace.

They knew only too well what this would mean to their little mission in Rangoon. Once word spread that the king had rejected their plea, even those few Burmans who had already come to Christ would be treated abominably — overtaxed, beaten, tortured or even killed — unless they renounced their newfound faith. No one else would come anywhere near the mission house to hear their message or receive copies of the literature that he and Ann had worked so hard to translate into Burmese so that the people could understand it. They had gambled on the king and lost. This would surely mean they would have to move the mission, perhaps out of Burma.

As they started on the voyage home, Adoniram prayed. "O Lord, at your leading we have toiled ceaselessly in this country of great tyranny to which you have sent us. And if we were able to see the end result of these efforts, as you can, I know that we would be compelled to give you the highest praise! Though I cannot now see it, please make my heart quicker to trust in the power and wisdom of my Almighty King, Christ Jesus. Please show your rule over all the world and defend your gospel in this small kingdom."

Even before Rangoon came into sight, Adoniram heard the temple bells on its many Buddhist pagodas tinkling in the wind. When they rounded the bend they saw their little group on the pier awaiting them—their wives and the three members of their mission church: Maung Nau, Maung Thahlah, and Maung Byaay. It was February 18th, 1820.

On Sunday, Adoniram called the tiny church together and explained all that had happened in Ava before the king. "We will have to close the mission now, or you will be in great danger. You may expect persecution and suffering if you stay, but you are all welcome to come with us to our next mission," Adoniram said sadly.

Almost in unison, the three Burman believers begged the Judsons not to leave. Every danger that Adoniram described, they made light of. This from men who a few months ago had begged not to be baptized in the daytime so as to avoid persecution much less severe than what they could now expect!

A few nights later, Maung Byaay came to the mission and asked to speak to Adoniram. "Teacher, I have been most distressed since you said you were leaving. I have found many more among my people who are examining the new religion. Some of them are close to the kingdom of God. Please stay until there are eight or ten disciples so that we can have a church that continues after you go. I know if we ask Him, God will raise up one among us to become teacher of the rest."

It seemed that the dark prospect of losing the gospel of Christ altogether was having a strong effect in Rangoon. The Judsons stayed until July 19, 1820, when they determined that Ann would have to spend a few months away because of illness. Nevertheless, as their ship sailed from Rangoon, Adoniram and Ann waved to a crowd of well-wishers on shore that included ten native Burman Christians. With all their hearts, the Judsons praised their own mighty King, Christ Jesus, whose power prevails over the fickle opposition of earthly rulers.

Today, hundreds of Burman Christians trace their spiritual roots back to the Judsons' tireless work in the nineteenth century. Despite tremendous persecution from the current regime in Burma, they hold to their faith, looking forward to their citizenship in Christ's eternal kingdom.

FROM THE BIBLE:

"You say that I am a king. For this purpose I was born and for this purpose I have come into the world — to bear witness to the truth. Everyone who is of the truth listens to my voice." (John 18:37b)

Who shall separate us from the love of Christ? Shall tribulation, or distress, or persecution, or famine, or nakedness, or danger, or sword? ... No, in all these things we are more than conquerors through him who loved us. (Romans 8:35, 37)

TALKING IT OVER:

1. *Was the spread of Christ's gospel thwarted by King Bagyidaw's rejection of the missionaries' petition, as Adoniram feared it would be?*

2. *How was Christ a king to the Burman Christians?*

3. *Where does Christ rule? How does He defend His Kingdom on earth today?*

THE TEN COMMANDMENTS

God's Moral Law

QUESTIONS TO LEARN:

64. **How many commandments did God give on Mount Sinai?**

Ten commandments.

65. **What are the Ten Commandments sometimes called?**

God's moral law.

66. **What do the first four commandments teach?**

Our duty to God.

67. **What do the last six commandments teach?**

Our duty to our fellow men.

*　　　　　*　　　　　*

In God's great mercy, He did not leave his fallen people ignorant of His holy standards, but gave them the Ten Commandments at a time when He was ready to lead them into a new life in a new land and ultimately to a Savior. Nine centuries after Christ, God led England's Alfred the Great to reintroduce those same righteous standards to another people who lived in great moral confusion.

Ten Lessons on Loving God

Moses rubbed his bleary eyes and took a sip of water, hoping it would revive him enough to finish this day's work. Over the heads of those crowding nearest to him, he heard several men bickering, but this was nothing new.

Shortly, Joshua approached him. He patted the tired Moses on the back and propped him up a bit. "Moses," he said, "Those two brothers-in-law, the ones who each claim ownership of the same twenty sheep, are next in line. Should I tell them to come back tomorrow?"

Moses sighed, exhausted from being God's only mouthpiece to the Israelite people. It was through Moses alone that God communicated how he wanted them to live. Day after day Moses labored to find out what God held as right and wrong in the various disputes the people brought to him.

"How many more are there, Joshua?"

"There are five men and two widows, three disputes in all. But Moses, the sun is almost behind Mount Sinai. I think it would be reasonable to send them home for today. You've been at it since daybreak, after all."

"Ah, but if I carry these over until tomorrow, I will have to carry even more over to the next day, and so on. No, Joshua, send over the brothers-in-law, and tell the others that I will get to them before I take my evening meal. But you could help me out by roasting a few quail over a fire for me."

The moon was glistening brightly by the time Moses had settled all the daily disputes of the people he had led out of Egypt at God's direction. He thanked the Lord for revealing His righteousness regarding the various issues they had brought before Him that day, and he prayed for the Israelites to know God's standards in their hearts. Then he silently, almost grimly, joined Joshua for a late supper.

It was not that Moses resented the people for their demands upon him. No, Moses had great compassion for these people God had given him to lead.

"They have been in darkness for such a long time," Moses thought, as he bit the tasty meat off a tiny bone. Until God had sent Moses and his brother, Aaron, to bring the Israelites out of Egypt, He had not spoken to his people for 400 years. During that time they had no written record of His promises *or* His laws. So they were mostly ignorant of what God expected of them and of how to be righteous! On top of that, they were enslaved and treated horribly by the Egyptians. Even now that God's mighty hand had delivered them and had lovingly provided for them time and again in this desert, they seemed unable to know how to live for Him. Moses longed for the day when all the people would learn God's ways without his own constant intervention.

The next afternoon Moses was surprised with a message from his father-in-law, Jethro, who was en route to Mount Sinai. Moses met him in the desert that evening and told him all that God had done in delivering the Israelites. Jethro rejoiced and stayed a few days at the mountain with Moses' family.

After observing life in the huge Israelite camp for a day or two, Jethro felt compelled to offer Moses a little fatherly advice. "Moses, what are you doing?" he cried. "You are going to kill yourself working at this pace. You can't hear and decide every single dispute yourself. Why, there must be 600,000 people in this camp, and they seem to know nothing about how to treat each other or their God.

"If God so commands, you need to teach *them* how to please Him. Why not set God-fearing, trustworthy men over them who know God's laws and can decide the disputes that the people can't settle for themselves? You can still hear the most difficult cases. This way you will bear up under the strain, and the people will be satisfied because they will know what to do."

Moses was encouraged by this counsel. It confirmed all that he had been praying for. "But how can I assign others to administer God's laws, when I don't know what all his laws are?" he asked himself.

Not long after this, the Lord Himself called Moses to meet Him on Mount Sinai to receive the specific laws and decrees that would teach the Israelites right from wrong. In the Ten Commandments, God set out his moral law for all people for all time.

Now the Israelites could know God's character for themselves and could understand how to treat one another in accordance with God's plan for mankind.

Each of these Ten Commandments was repeated and explained by Jesus during his earthly ministry, or by the apostles and others who wrote the books of the New Testament. In his grace and mercy, God gave fallen man these commands to teach us good from evil, to show us what it means to love Him, and to help us to live in harmony with other people.

(Taken from Exodus 18-21)

FROM THE BIBLE:

Fear God and keep his commandments, for this is the whole duty of man. For God will bring every deed into judgment, with every secret thing, whether good or evil. (Ecclesiastes 12:13b-14)

God ... appointed a law in Israel, which he commanded our fathers to teach their children, that the next generation might know them, the children yet unborn, and arise and tell them to their children, ... (Psalm 78:5b-6)

TALKING IT OVER:

1. *Who was the leader of the Israelites, Moses or God? Why do you say this?*

2. *Was it kind or harsh for God to put the Israelites under the Law? Why did they need the Ten Commandments?*

3. *Why do we need the Ten Commandments today?*

"Great" Is the Law

Alfred bent over several pages of Latin script and struggled to make out their meaning. His capable teacher, Asser, sat across the table patiently waiting for him to decipher the next phrase of the Bible. "Come, Alfred, you know these words. You can do it," the old priest urged him in the heavy Welsh accent that Alfred had come to love. During these sessions, Alfred put aside his British crown and became the humble student.

Just then a banging on the heavy wooden door of Alfred's chamber forced him to take up his crown once again. "Sire," said the assistant who entered, "Prince Edward and the Archbishop of Canterbury are asking to see you. They say it is urgent. There is more unrest in the countryside."

"Well, show them in immediately," Alfred ordered. "You stay too," he said to Asser, who was politely gathering his things to leave. "I might need your help."

Young Edward rushed in with the archbishop on his heels and gave his father a quick but respectful bow. "Sit, both of you," said Alfred. "What is your news?"

"Sire," said the archbishop, "it seems that the men in some of your counties are now totally out of control. They have been fighting increasingly amongst themselves ever since your armies pushed the enemy out of our territories a few years ago. To put it plainly, Sire, they are warriors, and they crave battle so much that they attack their own countrymen when no foreign foe can be found. They know nothing about how to live peaceably together."

"Why Father," Edward added, "they have barely even begun to rebuild their towns these past four years because they have been too busy killing and stealing from each other, and then

avenging those same crimes against their own kindred. These actions threaten the very survival of our kingdom!"

Alfred listened carefully to the dire predictions of his son and the archbishop of Canterbury. He could send his army out once again to attempt to subdue his lawless countrymen, but that strategy had not proven very effective so far. Each time he had put down such unrest, fresh tales of uprisings had reached the palace even before his men had returned home. No, something more was needed – much more. Alfred dismissed his high-ranking messengers to ponder the matter in the company of Asser.

"You know, old man," he said to his teacher, "we have been so long at war here in Wessex, that none of my subjects remembers what it is like to live in a stable world. Once we beat back the Danes and the Vikings, I was hopeful that we would have many years of peace ahead. But I myself am a creature of war, Asser. Besides threatening them, how can I help my people to be God-fearing and man-loving?"

"My king, I think that God has put the answer to that question right under your nose. You will find it if you take up your Scriptures and study Exodus. I will pray that you gain wisdom in this matter along with increased skill in Latin." And with that, Asser left him.

Over the next several days, Alfred toiled through Exodus, roughly translating the Latin into his native tongue of English. Of most interest to him was the story of God's gift of the Law to the

Israelites through Moses. Those Israelites were so like his own people! They had no concept of how to love God or one another. They seemed totally ignorant of their duties to anyone but themselves. Because of their need, God had given them the Ten Commandments.

"And that is precisely what my own people need," Alfred concluded. "I must tell them what standards of behavior they must meet. However, because I am sure to give them the wrong standards if I make them up on my own, I will begin with the same standards that God gave to Israel!"

In A.D. 890, King Alfred the Great of England issued his famous *Doombook* containing the righteous laws that he would enforce throughout his realm. In the introduction, Alfred stated that his laws were based on the Ten Commandments, which God gave to Moses, and which Jesus fulfilled and interpreted in love and compassion for mankind. Alfred demanded that under his law rich and poor would be judged alike. His *Doombook* even summarized the Bible's "golden rule," stating, "that which ye will that other men should not do to you, that do ye not to them."[1]

Under Alfred's reign, the English people enjoyed a period of peace and prosperity in the midst of many dark centuries of savagery, ignorance and confusion. He is the only king of England ever given the title "the Great."

---

1. P.J. Helm, *Alfred the Great* (New York: Thomas Y. Crowell Co., 1963), 111.

FROM THE BIBLE:

"Do not think that I have come to abolish the Law or the Prophets; I have not come to abolish them but to fulfill them. For truly, I say to you, until heaven and earth pass away, not an iota, not a dot, will pass from the Law until all is accomplished. Therefore whoever relaxes one of the least of these commandments and teaches others to do the same will be called least in the kingdom of heaven, but whoever does them and teaches them will be called great in the kingdom of heaven." (Matthew 5:17-19)

TALKING IT OVER:

1. *In light of Jesus' words quoted above, do you think it is appropriate for King Alfred to be called "the Great"? Do you think he is even greater in the kingdom of heaven?*

2. *Did God intend for all people in all ages to be subject to his moral law set out in the Ten Commandments? Why? (Because his moral standards apply to our whole world and not just to the Israelites. There is blessing for all people who obey them.)*

3. *Why is it good for God's law to be enacted as the law of a country, as Alfred did? (It benefits human relationships, as well as the relationships between human beings and God).*

Sum of the Commandments

Questions to learn:

68. **What is the sum of the Ten Commandments?**

To love God with all my heart, and my neighbor as myself.

69. **Who is your neighbor?**

All my fellow men are my neighbors.

70. **Is God pleased with those who love and obey Him?**

Yes. He says, "I love them that love me."

71. **Is God pleased with those who do not love and obey Him?**

No. "God is angry with the wicked every day."

*   *   *

Perhaps no biblical account so captures the spirit of the Ten Commandments as the touching story of Ruth's sacrifice of her family, customs and homeland in order to accompany her heartbroken mother-in-law, Naomi, back to Bethlehem. Another such servant of God was the English missionary Boniface, who toiled a lifetime to re-establish Christianity throughout heathen, eighth-century Europe, and who ultimately gained a martyr's crown.

"Your God Will Be My God"

"Ruth, tell me, I want to know what you are going to do?" demanded Orpah, as the two washed clothes in a stream that ran by their tent. Inside, their mother-in-law, Naomi, rested from their long journey toward Bethlehem.

"Are you going all the way to Bethlehem with Naomi, or are you coming back home with me to Moab?"

Ruth gazed downstream and imagined the Moabite valley in which her beloved village sprawled. She could have crossed that valley blindfolded, sensing by feel or sound or smell just when to turn up this or that path to the home of her parents or one of her many relatives. Was there a tree she hadn't watched grow taller? A child whose birth she had not celebrated? A death she hadn't grieved?

What, on the other hand, was in Bethlehem? Ruth didn't know. Only two things were for sure – Naomi was going there, and the people there followed Naomi's God.

"Naomi is right, you know," Orpah pressed. "You and I have no future in Bethlehem. In Moab there are men who will marry us since our Jewish husbands have died. These men have known us all our lives; we are their kind, and they'll take care of us. Perhaps we can finally have the children that Kilion and Mahlon were unable to give us. In Bethlehem, the men will have no use for two Moabite widows who may be barren. Go back with me and make a life for yourself, Ruth."

"And what of Naomi?" Ruth whispered. "What will she have if we let her return alone? She has lost her husband and both her sons. She left her friendships behind in Bethlehem ten long years ago. And she is too old to bear children, so no man will marry her either. How will she eat? Who will love her?"

"I know, I know, Ruth," Orpah answered, "but what can we do to help her? She is determined to go on, and we would just be two more mouths to feed. If we go back home, at least we can save ourselves."

After dinner that evening, Ruth took a walk alone. She remembered her last visit to the temple of Chemosh, the Moabite's most revered god, and how she had watched the townspeople continually going in and out. She recalled the many prayers she herself had offered to Chemosh in that very temple – trying to trust in the magical glistening of his sapphire eyes, the strength of his huge gold claws. Even as a child, however, doubt had nagged her when she had gone there. What could a hunk of gold do for her, no matter how beautifully it was cast? She had never even been able to detect a movement of this god, so how could he now give her children or even a joyful heart? She suspected that others wondered the same thing.

But Naomi's God, the God of Ruth's dead husband, Mahlon – this God seemed very different. For one thing, unlike Chemosh, he didn't live in a building. Moreover, Naomi worshipped Him not for riches, but for righteousness. He did not promise rain and crops, but forgiveness and redemption. He did not offer only power, but love. If Ruth let Naomi return to Bethlehem without her, would Ruth lose this God? Would a new husband make her bow before the cold, lifeless Chemosh and offer that lame god gifts in exchange for a son he had no power to give to her?

The next afternoon, Naomi announced to Ruth and Orpah that she would be ready to resume her journey to Bethlehem the next morning. "Let me be very clear, girls. I want you both to go back to your families and friends where I can be sure you'll be taken care of," Naomi said.

Orpah bitterly nodded and wept as Ruth stood watching.

Before the sun rose the next morning, Ruth got up quietly and washed her face in the stream. She dressed, pulled a small pack from under her mat,

and positioned herself at the tent's flap. Soon Naomi awoke and found her there, barring the way.

"You must let me go, child. I have to return to my people and my God," Naomi said, embracing her daughter-in-law tenderly.

But Ruth clung to her. "I am coming with you," she whispered.

"I thought we had settled this," Naomi said. "You must go back to your people, Ruth. Orpah is going. Go with her."

"Please don't urge me to go back without you, Naomi. I have made my decision. *Where you go I will go, and where you stay I will stay. Your people will be my people and your God my God. Where you die I will die, and there I will be buried. May the Lord deal with me, be it ever so severely, if anything but death separates you and me.*"

And so Ruth went on with her beloved Naomi. Before long, in Bethlehem, the Lord gave his servant Ruth a husband as gentle and self-sacrificing as she was herself. Together, Ruth and Boaz cared for Naomi as their own mother, and the Lord gave them a son whom they named Obed. Obed became the grandfather of King David, through whom God eventually gave us His own Son, Jesus Christ.

(Taken from Ruth 1 and 4)

FROM THE BIBLE:

Owe no one anything, except to love each other, for the one who loves another has fulfilled the law. The commandments, "You shall not commit adultery, You shall not murder, You shall not steal, You shall not covet," and any other commandment, are summed up in this word: "You shall love your neighbor as yourself." (Romans 13:8-9)

You shall love the Lord your God with all your heart and with all your soul and with all your might. (Deuteronomy 6:5)

TALKING IT OVER:

1. *Do you think that Ruth loved God with all her heart? How did she show her love?*

2. *Did Orpah love Naomi? What was the difference in how Orpah and Ruth loved Naomi? Which of them loved Naomi as she loved herself?*

3. *How did God show that He was pleased with Ruth's love and obedience? (See catechism question 70).*

The Law of Love

Lioba tried not to fret as she gathered the items she would need on her journey to see cousin Boniface at the monastery in Mainz. She found that a change of clothes, a loaf of bread for the evening meal, and the few chapters of Scripture she personally owned fit snugly into the small pail that she would use during the day as a purse and at night fill with water to soak her aching feet after the long day's walk. A nun in the year A.D. 752 did not have many needs.

"Why has my archbishop summoned me?" she asked Boniface's messenger, Winbrand, as she joined him in the courtyard of her abbey. "He does not say that it's urgent, and yet it's so unusual for him to call for me. Oh, I hope he is not ill! How could we continue the work without him?

"No, Sister, he is not ill," Winbrand assured her, "though I do believe his old bones grow weary of living. He said I could tell you that he has come to a decision he wishes to share with you. I can say no more. Are you ready?"

"Yes, by all means, Brother Winbrand. Let's not delay another moment," said Lioba, who turned and gave the sisters a few parting orders and then hurried out the gate.

By the time they had arrived in Mainz a few days later, Lioba was sure she had guessed what Boniface might tell her. "I believe he is retiring," she thought, but did not voice this to Winbrand. "He will finally take his rest at Fulda, his beloved monastery deep in the Bavarian forest. Well, all I can say is that he has certainly earned it! How long has he toiled throughout Europe, boldly but gently revealing Christ to the superstitious heathen? Thirty-five years, I think, maybe longer. All that, after leaving such a promising career in the English church where he could have been the leading scholar and teacher of our day. Yes, he will announce his much deserved retirement."

*   *   *

"Retirement!" roared Boniface when she let slip her suspicion to him. "My dear cousin, I will cease my toil when the Lord removes me from this earth and gives me eternal rest, not a moment before. Even then, I suspect there will be much more work to do. No, I am not retiring. In fact, I've called you here to tell you I'm returning to Frisia where our mission has grown cold and fruitless. So very many there are in need of our Savior."

"Frisia!" She shot back. "Oh, but there are younger men whom you could send, Boniface. Please consider your age and the dangers. You know that the heathen tribes on the north shore have long been some of the most savage and cold-hearted in all of Europe."

"I fully expect to die there, Lioba. But do not worry. There is no other way I'd rather go to my Lord than while shouting his name in a dark land.

You must promise me that you too will work hard to your last day here in the land we've adopted at Christ's direction. Don't grow weary, and don't despair of your long life. Remember how very much longer eternity will be. Now, tell them to bury me at Fulda, and to bury you next to me one day so that we can enjoy the resurrection together. Goodbye my sister in Christ."

* * *

Lioba returned to her abbey deeply encouraged by the words and deeds of Boniface. Each evening at vespers she led her nuns in praying for his mission in Frisia, and during the days she often prayed for him privately as she went about her work. A year passed, and then two.

Finally Lioba received a correspondence she had been expecting. Her old friend Winbrand brought it personally and placed it gently into her hand. It was from Lul, whom Boniface had appointed to succeed him at Mainz:

> My dear Sister, I am at once grieved and overjoyed to inform you that Boniface, our beloved brother in Christ, has died a martyr's death at the hand of those he sought to save. I do not have to describe to you the courage and love that he showed in his last moments, for you know him even better than I. Before his end, though, he preached to thousands, destroyed numerous pagan altars, and constructed many churches for our Lord. We have also learned that a large number of the pagans for whom he toiled have come to know Christ even since his death. Please come and pay your last respects. Lul.

Once more Lioba packed for Mainz, this time with a lighter heart – a heart inspired to love God and others at all costs. "He finally got that retirement," she thought. "How glorious it must be!"

FROM THE BIBLE:

Love does no wrong to a neighbor; therefore love is the fulfilling of the law. (Romans 13:10)

Do nothing from rivalry or conceit, but in humility count others more significant than yourselves. Let each of you look not only to his own interests, but also to the interests of others. Have this mind among yourselves, which is yours in Christ Jesus, who, though he was in the form of God, did not count equality with God a thing to be grasped, but made himself nothing, taking the form of a servant, … (Philippians 2:3-7a)

TALKING IT OVER:

1. *Do you think Boniface obeyed God's moral law? How? (See the verse from Romans above.)*

2. *How did Boniface show that he loved his neighbors as himself?*

3. *Who were Boniface's neighbors?*

4. *How do you think God showed that He was pleased with Boniface's love and obedience to Him? (Through the assurance of eternal life, his joy and peace, and the success of his mission).*

Unit 5 – Section 3
Love God with All Your Heart

QUESTIONS TO LEARN:

72. What is the first commandment?

The first commandment is, "Thou shalt have no other gods before me."

73. What does the first commandment teach us?

To worship God only.

74. What is the second commandment?

The second commandment is, "Thou shalt not make unto thee any graven image, or any likeness of anything that is in heaven above, or that is in the earth beneath, or that is in the water under the earth: thou shalt not bow down thyself to them: for I, the LORD thy God, am a jealous God, visiting the iniquity of the fathers upon the children unto the third and fourth generation of them that hate me; and showing mercy unto thousands of them that love me and keep my commandments."

75. What does the second commandment teach us?

To worship God in the right way, and to avoid idolatry.

76. **What is the third commandment?**

The third commandment is, "Thou shalt not take the name of the LORD thy God in vain; for the LORD will not hold him guiltless that taketh His name in vain."

77. **What does the third commandment teach us?**

To reverence God's name, word, and works.

*　　　　　*　　　　　*

The first three commandments talk about our duty to give God first place in our hearts and lives. When the Israelites under King Ahab worshipped the pagan idol Baal, God mercifully sent his prophet Elijah to direct their attention back to worship the one true God alone. Four centuries after Christ, God convicted Jerome of his more subtle worship of pagan philosophers, later using him to write the translation of the Bible that was relied on for the next eleven hundred years.

Fire on the Mount

"Jezebel, it wasn't like what you are thinking," whined King Ahab to his livid wife, an iron-willed woman with a cruel streak as wide as the Jordan River. "I didn't *invite* Elijah to make fools of our gods – Baal and Asherah. What happened is that he showed up in Samaria making what sounded like wild claims about his God being able to end the drought that has caused this long famine. I was sure our starving people would revolt if I didn't shut him up. That's when he made me an offer I couldn't refuse."

"Oh," Jezebel trembled in fury, "did he offer you some common sense?"

"Listen," Ahab wheedled, "Elijah was willing to single-handedly go up against all 450 of the prophets of Baal and all 400 prophets of Asherah, on Mount Carmel. In such a contest, with the odds so strongly in our favor, it simply didn't seem possible for the ancient God of my forefathers to outshine Baal!"

"He didn't just 'outshine' Baal, you fool. He put to death all 450 of my … I mean Baal's prophets! How will we ever convince the people that Baal deserves their worship now?" Jezebel demanded, lifting her hand contemptuously.

"But Elijah gave the prophets plenty of opportunity to demonstrate the power of Baal to the people first," Ahab contended, surprising himself. "It was really an amazing display. There we were on the mountain before the thousands of Israelites that I had called together to prove the strength of Baal. Elijah stood before this crowd and asked, *'How long will you waver between two opinions? If the* LORD *is God, follow him; but if Baal is God, follow him.'* This seemed a most reasonable suggestion to everyone. So to help them decide whom to follow, Elijah presented his challenge.

"At his suggestion, your 450 prophets selected the choicest bull and prepared it as a sacrifice to Baal. They placed the bull on Baal's altar and prayed from morning till noon asking him to set the sacrifice on fire. But nothing happened, Jezebel. The people began to grumble, urging the prophets on in their antics until they were dancing around the altar, working themselves up into fits. They even cut their own bodies with spears in order to please Baal. Still the wood lay cold beneath the bull.

"Elijah didn't say a word until afternoon, when he asked Baal's prophets if their gods might be too busy to answer them. 'Perhaps he is tied up thinking or sleeping, or maybe he's on vacation.' Elijah suggested. This secretly pleased me because I knew that Elijah's arrogance would make the people all the more bloodthirsty when his God, too, was unable or unwilling to light the sacrificial fire. I thought that Baal could still win.

"When the 450 finally gave up their prophesying, Elijah regathered the people who had by then drifted away. He rebuilt the ruined altar that my ancestors once used to worship his God. He made sure everybody saw that he constructed it out of twelve stones, supposedly representing the twelve tribes of Israel talked about in all the old legends. Then he prepared a bull of his own, arranged the wood, and put the bull on it. But what he did next was the most shocking.

"He had the people soak the bull and the wood beneath it three times, until water filled the trench around the altar. At this point I was elated, Jezebel.

I savored the moment Elijah's proud test would explode in his face. That would teach him to taunt Baal!

"I expected him to make some dramatic display that would rival that of Baal's prophets, but instead he just stood there before the soggy sacrifice and prayed, 'O Lord, God of Abraham, Isaac, and Israel, show these people that you are their God, that I am your servant, and that I have done all these things today at your command. Answer me, O Lord, so that these people will know that you are turning their hearts back to you again.'

"Jezebel, the Lord's fire fell instantly on Elijah's sacrifice, consuming the wood, the bull, the stones, the soil, and even the water in the trench! The people fell to the ground at this display of God's power and worshipped Him as the one true God. It was all I could do not to join them. Then they helped Elijah put Baal's prophets to death for their deceit.

"Not long after that, the rain began. Perhaps we should bow to the Lord while we are still able, Jezebel," Ahab concluded.

"I will never bow down," Jezebel snarled. "Messenger!" she screamed at a cowering servant, "find Elijah and say to him: 'May the gods deal with me, be it ever so severely, if by this time tomorrow I do not make your life like that of Baal's prophets whom you killed.' We will yet show the people Baal's power and majesty!"

But again God displayed his power. In time, it was Jezebel, not Elijah, who forfeited her life in a futile battle against the one true God.

(Taken from 1 Kings 18:16-19:2; 2 Kings 9:30-37)

FROM THE BIBLE:

"I am the Lord, and there is no other, besides me there is no God; I equip you, though you do not know me, that people may know, from the rising of the sun and from the west, that there is none besides me; I am the Lord, and there is no other." (Isaiah 45:5-6)

"To whom will you liken me and make me equal ... ? Those who lavish gold from the purse, and weigh out silver in the scales, hire a goldsmith, and he makes it into a god; then they fall down and worship! ... If one cries to it, it does not answer or save him from his trouble. Remember this and stand firm, recall it to mind, you transgressors, remember the former things of old; for I am God, and there is no other; I am God, and there is none like me." (Isaiah 46:5a, 6, and 7b-9)

TALKING IT OVER:

1. Were the Israelites worshipping God only? What was the result of their failure to do so?

2. How did God show that He was the one and only true God? Based on what God taught the people of Israel on Mount Carmel, does it surprise you that Jezebel's gods did not help her to kill Elijah, as she vowed, but that God instead delivered Elijah, and put Jezebel and Ahab to death for leading the people into idolatry?

3. If we are worshipping God alone, how will that show in our lives? (We will have boldness like Elijah had; we will pray to God, and we will trust his power).

A Slave to What
Masters You

Engrossed in an urgent letter he was dictating to the bishop of Rome, Evagrios had asked not to be disturbed. He was quite surprised, therefore, when a servant tapped on his study door and begged him to come out and tend to a visitor who had just arrived. He was even more surprised to find a familiar young man on his doorstep, swaying with fatigue, or illness, or both.

Evagrios rushed forward, catching his friend just before he fell, and half carried him to a chair in the entryway. "Jerome!" he cried delightedly. "You have finally come east to join the desert monks in their wholehearted devotion to Christ. I knew you would do it one day."

As he talked, Evagrios poured some water between Jerome's parched lips. He wondered why his intellectual friend had chosen to make the difficult journey to Antioch in the middle of the summer – always brutal in and around Syria. Surely he had not attempted it alone.

A braying from the front yard assured Evagrios that Jerome had company. There stood three exhausted servants and six large donkeys about to buckle under the heat and the tremendous weight of their burdens. "Jerome, my friend," Evagrios laughed, "have you brought your whole household with you to make the Syrian desert more comfortable? I'm not sure you have quite grasped the spirit of true devotion."

"Why, I haven't brought luxuries," Jerome sputtered in his own defense. "These are simply my books. I've copied them all myself, and I, I … I just couldn't entrust them to anyone else."

Evagrios silently peered back at Jerome. "I think I understand perfectly, my friend," he thought. "I guess you are not ready to meet with God in the desert just yet. Well, perhaps in Antioch God will claim your full affection."

Under Evagrios' gentle and generous care, Jerome slowly regained his physical strength over the next several months. But Evagrios could see that Jerome was still very, very sick emotionally and spiritually. Almost daily, Jerome slipped out, went into the city, and indulged himself in Greek lessons. He quite often debated with Antioch's scholars regarding the finer points of Greek and Roman philosophy, science, and literature, none of which acknowledged the existence of the true God. On these days Jerome returned home elated, but soon grew despondent. Evagrios saw how Jerome ached to be able to leave the world behind and devote himself to the solitary lifestyle of a monk – a life of constant prayer, fasting, and study of Scripture. But Jerome was still far from willing. So Evagrios prayed often for his friend.

Frequently when Jerome had fallen into one of his dark moods, he would announce rather early in the evening that he was retiring to study some particular book of the Bible. More often than not, however, Evagrios found Jerome the next morning asleep over one of his favorite passages of Cicero or Virgil rather than the Old Testament prophets that Jerome claimed to be studying. Once when Evagrios found him this way, Jerome awoke and confessed tearfully, "I grieved over the awkward language of these Latin translations of the Bible and longed to read something truly beautiful."

In time, Jerome fell ill with a fever that had already claimed the lives of many in Antioch. One evening while Evagrios prayed by his bedside, Jerome pitched and thrashed in his delirium more than usual. He cried out in his sleep, "I am a Christian!" And then he sobbed for several minutes before he sank into a restful slumber.

The next morning, Jerome's fever had broken. He was still very weak, but gone were the anxious lines that Evagrios had recently seen etched deep into Jerome's brow. "What happened, Jerome? Last night I watched a man in anguish of soul."

Jerome answered quietly, "In my sleep I was dragged before the Judge of heaven and earth, who was surrounded by a light so dazzling that it forced me to cover my eyes and crawl along the ground before him. 'What religion are you?' the Judge demanded of me. Without hesitation, I answered, 'I am a Christian.' But from the bench I heard him cry, 'That is a lie. You worship Cicero, not Christ. You take Christ's name, but he is not really your God. Thus, you take his name in vain. Where your treasure is, there your heart is also!'

"I knew instantly that his verdict was true. I was an idolater. And my remorse tormented me more than the lashes that the accuser in my dream ordered to be inflicted upon me. After a time I begged for mercy, and many present there also asked for mercy on my behalf. I promised that henceforth I would put God first and seek after his true beauty. I would no longer worship Cicero and Virgil – those pagan illusions of beauty. I was given mercy. Evagrios, I think that after I am a little stronger, I will leave for the desert."

In the rugged caves of the Syrian desert, Jerome's love for God grew stronger than any love he had ever known. There he also learned Hebrew from a Jewish Christian monk. With his knowledge of God and languages, Jerome soon gave the world a Latin translation of the Bible that was more beautifully written, and that was truer to the original manuscripts, than any other Latin translation in existence at that time.

FROM THE BIBLE:

"For it is written, 'You shall worship the Lord your God and him only shall you serve.'" (Matthew 4:10b)

"No one can serve two masters, for either he will hate the one and love the other, or he will be devoted to the one and despise the other. You cannot serve God and money." (Matthew 6:24)

TALKING IT OVER:

1. *When God tells us in the first commandment to have no other gods before him, "other gods" include false gods like Buddha and Allah, who are worshipped in today's world. God showed Jerome that "other gods"*

also includes anything that we are tempted to put before God. What was Jerome's "other god"?

2. *Is it wrong to care about things in the world? When is it wrong? (When something else comes before God, or our desire for something else interferes with our desire for God, or our esteem for something else rises to the level of worship).*

3. *Do you have any "other gods"? What are they? What will you do about them?*

4. *Did Jerome genuinely reverence God's name, word, and works? Why do you think so? (Consider different periods of his life).*

The Lord's Day

Questions to learn:

78. **What is the fourth commandment?**

    The fourth commandment is, "Remember the Sabbath day to keep it holy. Six days shalt thou labor, and do all thy work: but the seventh day is the Sabbath of the Lord thy God: in it thou shalt not do any work, thou, nor thy son, nor thy daughter, nor thy manservant, nor thy maidservant, nor thy cattle, nor thy stranger that is within thy gates: for in six days the LORD made heaven and earth, the sea and all that in them is, and rested the seventh day: wherefore the LORD blessed the Sabbath day, and hallowed it."

79. **What does the fourth commandment teach us?**

    To keep the Sabbath holy.

80. **What day of the week is the Christian Sabbath?**

    The first day of the week, called the Lord's Day.

81. **Why is it called the Lord's Day?**

    Because on that day Christ rose from the dead.

82. **How should the Sabbath be kept?**

    In prayer and praise, in hearing and reading God's Word, and in doing good to our fellow men.

*   *   *

For many in Jesus' day, the Sabbath was simply an exercise in following trivial rules and elaborate rituals. But Jesus emphasized God's purposes for the Sabbath – resting, doing good to others, and honoring God. In this story, Jesus heals the shriveled hand of a worshipper, bringing him hope and joy on the Sabbath. Newspaperman Robert Raikes took the lessons of Jesus to heart when he helped start a Sunday school for illiterate children who worked six long days a week in England's early factories.

Lawful to Do Good

The synagogue was already abuzz very early on the Sabbath morning when the stranger with the crippled hand arrived in Capernaum. By sunrise, he had come almost the entire distance that a faithful Jew was allowed to walk on the Sabbath – three quarters of a mile. Joining the throng of Jews streaming toward the synagogue, he was relieved to learn that Jesus was still in town and would be speaking to the people about the amazing things of God that he had already heard so much about.

As he neared the door, the stranger saw that some of the elders stood by attentively, eyeing each person who entered. They seemed to be looking for someone. When he reached them, they peered at him closely, particularly when they noticed that his right hand was just a shriveled claw. Two of the elders who stared at the useless limb exchanged knowing looks, and the stranger even thought he saw a slight smile pass between them. They began ordering the other worshippers to move aside, and the stranger suddenly found himself being escorted to the very front row of the synagogue where the people already seated were shuffled around and squished together to make room for him.

The stranger gladly took this unexpected seat and settled in to wait for Jesus. Meanwhile the elders – now perched on the bench just across the aisle from him – kept whispering and nodding his way.

While the rest of the worshippers were still crowding into the synagogue, a man approached the crippled stranger from the other side, and surprised him with the command, "Stand here in front of everyone." Before the cripple could protest, the man reached out and took his dangling and withered right hand. It was Jesus.

So the cripple stood up next to Jesus, before the elders and all the people. Instantly, the buzz throughout the synagogue hushed. All eyes fixed on the limp hand that hung from his right sleeve. The elders who had seated him smiled up at them smugly.

"Which is lawful on the Sabbath: to do good or to do evil, to save life or to kill?" Jesus demanded of the silent crowd. No one said a word. Even the elders were speechless, their smirks quickly giving way to confusion.

Jesus gazed around the synagogue waiting for an answer to his question, but none came. The cripple saw the fire in his eyes when Jesus turned to him and said, *"Stretch out your hand."*

Shaking with anticipation, the crippled man obeyed and was thrilled to find a normal, useful, five-fingered hand at the end of his trembling right arm. He could *feel* it! He could move it for the first time in his life!

Seeing this, the elders rose and stormed out of the synagogue in a rage. But the people were amazed by the Lord's teaching. On this occasion and many others, Jesus showed the people that it is lawful to do good on the Sabbath, whether or not someone chooses to label it "work." He said that God had given men the Sabbath as a gift – a day of rest and a day to be devoted to God. The day itself should not be worshipped, but should be enjoyed by men for the purposes for which God gave it – to worship God, to do good, to rest from hard work and allow others to do so also.

The people were overjoyed at this teaching because trying to keep the many rules and regulations the Pharisees made for the Sabbath had come to feel more like work than rest, more like a burden than a gift. No one thought much about doing good on that day because they were so focused on following the procedures that would keep them out of trouble!

The newly healed stranger was brimming with joy when he left the synagogue in Capernaum. It had certainly been one of the best Sabbaths of his life! As he headed for a nearby inn, however, he saw the elders slipping into a home on the outskirts of town. He did not think they had appreciated one bit the spin Jesus had put on their Sabbath rules. "And yet, what goodness I have received today!" he marveled, as he gazed at his new fingers, supple with movement and life.

(Taken from Matthew 12:9-14; Mark 3:1-6; Luke 6:6-11, 13:10-17, 14:1-6; Deuteronomy 5:12-15)

FROM THE BIBLE:

And [Jesus] said to them, "The Sabbath was made for man, not man for the Sabbath. So the Son of Man is lord even of the Sabbath." (Mark 2:27-28)

TALKING IT OVER:

1. *From this story, how did Jesus keep the Sabbath?*

2. *Give some examples of ways you can keep the Lord's Day holy.*

Saved from a Sunday Whipping

Johnny Lambert slipped into the kitchen through the back door of his family's cottage with his usual care, knocking over the jug his mum had put out for him to take to the milk cart and fill. No, his mates from the pin factory did not call him "Stiff" for nothing. Unfortunately, this was not Johnny's first misstep of the day.

"Boy!" his dad bellowed from the only other room in the cramped little Lambert hovel. "Pick up that jug and get in here right now. I've somethin' to say to you!"

As Johnny scrambled across the kitchen floor retrieving the milk jug, he peered in through the doorway and tried to guess his father's state of mind. Sundays were always a little tense because his dad mostly spent them at one of Gloucester's many alehouses, drowning his misery with other overworked and underpaid factory workers. Sometimes when he got home, he was meaner than usual. Johnny took a few deep breaths, set his jaw, and went in to face his dad.

"That reverend from over at St. John's Church was by here this afternoon, boy," Johnny's father said sharply. "He says he thinks he spotted you settin' fire to a farmer's tool shed while those boys you run with stole as many o' his potatoes as they could carry. I don't haf to ask you if that's so," he declared, turning Johnny's hands up to expose his palms still smeared with ashes.

"You know, boy, I really don' care what you do, but if they put you in the jail, we'll lose your wages from the pin factory. It's hard enough for me'n your mum to feed your eight cheepin' little mouths every day without that bad luck on top of it.

"So you listen close now. The reverend made me a deal. He said he won' repeat his suspicions to the authorities if you and your bunch volunteer to rebuild that farmer's shed, and if you get yourselves to that Sunday school he and Mr. Raikes just got going so that you factory kids can learn to read and find out what's in the Bible. They're hopin' that'll keep you out of people's fields and off the streets on Sundays. Now what do you think of that?" asked his dad with a sidewise scowl that told Johnny what his answer had better be.

So relieved was he not to be dragged out into the yard and whipped, that Johnny didn't dream of complaining. In fact, his heart skipped just a beat or two faster. He was going to learn to read!

"And they're gonna take you to church too," his father warned, "so let's not hear any lip about that either. We need those pin factory wages, boy. You're the biggest of my ragamuffins and ya' bring home the most, pittance that it is."

The next Sunday morning, Mr. Raikes himself came around to gather Johnny into the little band of boys he was escorting to Sunday school. As the publisher of the county newspaper, the *Gloucester Journal*, Mr. Raikes was perhaps the most respected man in town. He cut a very fine form, there on the Lambert doorstep with all of Johnny's cohorts lined up behind him with clean faces, clean hands, and even combed hair! Mr. Raikes wouldn't let Johnny join their ranks until he was equally presentable, and then off they trooped to Mrs. Critchley's schoolroom.

Sundays were now a joy to Johnny Lambert. For six days a week he lived in his old world of twelve-hour workdays, frequent beatings, and meager meals that left him still feeling hollow inside. But on Sundays he miraculously entered the world of words, history, and God's love and provision for mankind. Reverend Stock preached that God had mercy even on those who'd done as bad as Johnny had and had sent his Son to prove it by paying the price for their wicked deeds. It reminded Johnny of the punishment he'd gotten for burning down the farmer's shed – not a whipping, but a Savior!

Johnny was so amazed by what he learned at Mr. Raikes' Sunday school and in Reverend Stock's sermons, that when his dad came in from the alehouse late on Sunday afternoons, he couldn't help telling him all about it. At first his dad didn't say anything when he went on and on about this or that bit of truth he'd found out. But after a time, his dad started to ask a question here and there, and soon Johnny noticed that he came in smelling less strongly of liquor.

One day his dad was already there when Johnny got home from Sunday school. "Come over here and tell me what you learned today, boy," he said.

After that his father was always there waiting for Johnny on Sunday afternoons. He seemed to get more comfort from what Johnny's Bible said than he used to get from cursing and drinking with his chums. Now Sunday was a day of rest and peace in Johnny's home.

Mr. Raikes and Reverend Stock's Sunday schools – started in 1780 when England's lower-class workers were being driven from the farms into the factories – were not the first of their kind. But Mr. Raikes used his considerable influence to widely promote the benefits of educating the poor in spiritual and moral matters. Soon the Sunday School Movement became popular within England and spread to America. What better way to honor God on His day, after all?

FROM THE BIBLE:

"If you turn back your foot from the Sabbath, from doing your pleasure on my holy day, and call the Sabbath a delight and the holy day of the Lord honorable; if you honor it, not going your own ways, or seeking your own pleasure, or talking idly; then you shall take delight in the Lord, … (Isaiah 58:13-14a)

TALKING IT OVER:

1. *What do you think it means to keep the Sabbath holy?*

2. *How did Mr. Raikes keep the Lord's Day? How did Johnny and his father keep the Lord's Day?*

3. *Why do you think God gave this command to his people?*

Love Others

83. **What is the fifth commandment?**

The fifth commandment is, "Honor thy father and thy mother that thy days may be long upon the land which the LORD thy God giveth thee."

84. **What does the fifth commandment teach us?**

To love and obey our parents.

85. **What is the sixth commandment?**

The sixth commandment is, "Thou shalt not kill."

86. **What does the sixth commandment teach us?**

To avoid hatred.

87. **What is the seventh commandment?**

The seventh commandment is, "Thou shalt not commit adultery."

88. **What does the seventh commandment teach us?**

To be pure in heart, language, and conduct.

89. **What is the eighth commandment?**

The eighth commandment is, "Thou shalt not steal."

90. **What does the eighth commandment teach us?**

To be honest and not to take the things of others.

91. **What is the ninth commandment?**

The ninth commandment is, "Thou shalt not bear false witness against thy neighbor."

92. **What does the ninth commandment teach us?**

To tell the truth and not to speak evil of others.

93. **What is the tenth commandment?**

The tenth commandment is, "Thou shalt not covet thy neighbor's house, thou shalt not covet thy neighbor's wife, nor his manservant, nor his maidservant, nor his ox, nor his ass, or anything that is thy neighbor's."

94. **What does the tenth commandment teach us?**

To be content with what we have.

* * *

In the last six commandments, God teaches us how to love others as ourselves. The two stories in this section show that our fulfillment of the last six commands is dependent upon whether we first love God with all our hearts, minds, and souls. When David's love for God waned, sin toward his fellow man was crouching at the door. Communist China, which from its inception has officially denied and discredited the one true God, in 1966 ushered in a "Cultural Revolution" in which the Chinese people were led to commit horrendous crimes specifically forbidden by the Ten Commandments.

Sin Crouches at the Door

When the sleeping Nathan heard a voice call to him out of the darkness, he knew enough to willingly depart his dreams and open his eyes. As one of the Lord's prophets, Nathan had learned long ago that he must listen whenever God spoke to him.

"Nathan, go to my servant King David and tell him that I am much displeased with him," said the voice.

"What shall I say has displeased you, Lord?" asked Nathan.

"He has taken the wife of his loyal servant Uriah for his own, and then arranged for Uriah to be killed in battle in order to cover up his evil deeds. He has broken and despised my holy laws and done a great evil before my eyes. You must tell him that I will punish him severely for this!"

"Yes, Lord, I will go to him," Nathan said.

Nathan did not return to his dreams that night. He thought instead about his wayward king – his beloved David, who had once been a man "after God's own heart." What had happened to him?

David had been so dependent on God during the many years he had waited patiently for his kingdom – the years during which the deranged

King Saul had repeatedly hunted him down and tried to kill him. But the Lord had protected David from these dangers, and David had trusted God to the point of sparing his enemy's life on more than one occasion, sure that God would fulfill his promises in His own way.

Once on his throne, David had taken his duties to God and his people very seriously, seeking to glorify God in all he did. He had steadfastly led his people in humble and joyful worship of God according to the directives of the Law, and he'd courageously led his armies to vanquish God's enemies again and again. The Lord had been with David through it all.

But recently, David just wasn't the same man. He had grown weary of battle, opting to stay home idly while his troops fought without him. And his loyalties seemed to have shifted a bit. Nathan wondered, for example, if David held his sons too close to his heart. Once God is displaced as our first love, all manner of evil has room to wriggle in and deceive us. These evils were much more dangerous to David than Saul ever was. Is this what had happened to him?

Well, it was not for Nathan to understand why. He had a message to deliver, and as soon as the sun crept over the horizon, he went forth to do just that.

"What brings you here so early in the day, Nathan?" asked a curious David as Nathan interrupted the breakfast he shared with his newest wife, Bathsheba, who was nursing their infant son. Bathsheba had once been married to Uriah.

"I must report something to you, Sire," Nathan said. David nodded his consent, and Nathan continued: "In a certain town there lived two men – one rich and the other poor. The poor man had a single ewe lamb he had bought with all of his savings. He raised it and cherished it like a child. The rich man, who had great flocks of sheep, was visited one day by a hungry traveler. Rather than butchering one of his own flock to provide the meal, however, the rich man seized the poor man's ewe and fed it to the traveler."

"Why, that's an outrage," David thundered as soon as Nathan had finished his tale. "That greedy, heartless man deserves to die! But first I will make

him pay for that lamb four times over. Who is this man?"

"*You are the man!*" Nathan said solemnly. "The Lord sent me to say to you: 'I have given you all that your heart could desire, yet you stole what belonged to your loyal servant Uriah, and then murdered him with the sword of the Ammonites. Now, therefore, I am going to bring calamity upon you and your household.'"

When David heard these words, Nathan saw that his heart was broken. David's anger continued to burn, but now toward himself. "I have sinned against my Lord," he acknowledged humbly. Never, in all the years he had loved and followed God, had he ever done such a thing against Him. He fell to the floor weeping.

"*The Lord has taken away your sin,*" Nathan told his repentant king. "You are forgiven; you will not die. But your actions have caused God's enemies to have contempt for him, therefore your son by this wrongful union will die."

For seven days, David fasted at the bedside of his stricken baby son, pleading with God. Each night he lay on the ground and would not move. He prayed: "*Against you, you only, have I sinned and done what is evil in your sight, so that you are proved right when you speak and justified when you judge. . . . Create in me a pure heart, O God, and renew a steadfast spirit within me. Do not cast me from your presence or take your Holy Spirit from me. Restore to me the joy of your salvation and grant me a willing spirit, to sustain me.*"

When the baby died, King David went to the temple and worshipped the righteous God who was faithful to His own commands and brought His people ever back to them.

(Taken from 2 Samuel 12; Psalm 51)

FROM THE BIBLE:

For you were called to freedom, brothers. Only do not use your freedom as an opportunity for the flesh, but through love serve one another. For the whole law is fulfilled in one word: "You shall love your neighbor as yourself." (Galatians 5:13-14)

"And if you do not do well, sin is crouching at the door. Its desire is for you, but you must rule over it." (Genesis 4:7b)

If we say we have no sin, we deceive ourselves, and the truth is not in us. If we confess our sins, he is faithful and just to forgive us our sins and to cleanse us from all unrighteousness. (1 John 1:8-9)

TALKING IT OVER:

1. *Look at the list of the Ten Commandments in catechism questions 72-94. Which of these did David violate in the above story?*

2. *What do you learn from this story about the relation of one sin to another? Can you recall a time when you committed a sin that led to another sin, and another, in succession? (David's coveting led to adultery, which led to murder.)*

3. *Where did David first go wrong? (He stopped focusing on pleasing God.)*

Confessions of a Red Guard Youth

August 18, 1966, is a date I will never forget for as long as I live. On that day, as an innocent, bright-eyed 16-year-old, I became one of Chairman Mao Zedong's "Red Guards." Mao was the communist leader of China from 1949 until he died in 1976. For the youths who became his "Red Guards" in 1966, Mao was god.

Two days before, on August 16, I said goodbye to my parents and told them I would return to them when I could. Joining my school friends, I walked and hitchhiked for forty straight hours from my hometown to reach Peking's Tiananmen Square in time to join in the first group of Red Guards that was reviewed by Chairman Mao. Along with us, thousands of other excited youth filled the square, all wearing red armbands to signify that we belonged to Mao and would do anything he told us to. Each of us carried a book of Mao's quotations, which we had been diligently memorizing so that we could know all that is important and good to believe. When he appeared before us on that fateful summer day, we showed our total trust in Chairman Mao by cheering until our voices gave out.

Then we all trekked back to our homes, hoping for opportunities to demonstrate our total trust in Chairman Mao. During the following days, my friends and I put up posters all over our town with Chairman Mao's quotations on them. We wore uniforms and carried red flags. Many of us stole weapons and carried those too. Chairman Mao had told us to wipe out anything and anyone that did not worship him completely. Such people and activities were labeled "counter-revolutionary." We were to investigate every such hint of disloyalty to him.

On one of my first days back home, I heard about a group of Red Guards who were tearing apart a church not far from my house. Because the few people who went to church in our society worshipped God rather than Mao, we realized that anyone we found in a church was automatically a "counter-revolutionary." Eager to do my part for Mao, I hurried over to the church to help. But all the windows had already been smashed and the altar had been set on fire. Several of the younger boys had found a minister inside the church, and they'd tied him up so that he was forced to watch all that we were doing.

Feeling a mighty surge of adrenaline at the sight of this helpless preacher, I fearlessly began to scale the steeple of the church with my eye on the only thing still intact – the cross on top. I seemed to reach it without any effort, and when a friend coming up just behind me handed me an ax, I hacked that cross until I finally managed to topple it to the ground. Those watching me from below wholeheartedly cheered this feat, and I stood atop that crossless steeple with my hands on my hips and believed that I had done something heroic for my beloved Mao. From then on, churches were a favorite target.

After a while, we were sent out to arrest people for specific "crimes" against Mao. All the townspeople had been ordered to think hard and inform authorities of anything unusual or suspicious that they noticed about anyone else. Informants emerged from every corner – some settling old grudges, some hoping that by pointing

the finger at their neighbors or coworkers they would keep suspicion off themselves, and others truly hoping to further Mao's cause by stamping out all disloyalty.

It was our job, as Red Guards, to force the accused to confess their crimes in front of angry screaming crowds that we assembled for this purpose. If they would not admit to whatever we charged them with, we beat them until they did. Those who survived the beatings were sentenced to death or to many years of hard labor in far-away prison camps. We never considered whether the charges we forced people to confess might be untrue.

One day I was summoned to a place where we held these meetings, and I found my own parents tied up before a crowd of accusers. I was told that a CB radio had been found at their house, and one of my father's work associates claimed that my father was a spy who had used the radio to send messages to foreign governments. Although I knew that playing with electronic gadgets was a hobby of my father's, I did not question the claims of his tormentors. "How dare he pretend to be trifling with radios while he is really plotting against Mao!" I thought.

Before I could act, however, the crowd turned on me because I was the son of the criminals. The leader of our Red Guard group, who liked me, quickly pulled me aside and told me that I could save myself if I immediately cut all ties with my parents and denounced them as traitors and criminals. He didn't have to convince me. I already hated them for bringing this dishonor upon me. I went to the front and screamed at them, "You are filthy scum who have put our Chairman Mao in peril. You are no longer, and never will be my parents." Then I spat on them and walked out.

My parents were sent to separate prison camps for the rest of the "Cultural Revolution." This is the name Mao gave to his ten-year campaign to keep his harsh, powerful hold over our people and our government.

After Mao died, people began to realize that what had happened during the Cultural Revolution in China was the worst sort of evil. My father died in prison from the unbearable conditions, or perhaps from a broken heart, but my mother was released and returned to our home in 1978. Eventually, she managed to restore my father's reputation by proving that the business associate who had accused him really had no information indicating that Father was a spy. This man was simply jealous that my father had once gotten a promotion that the man wanted for himself.

As for me, I had denounced my father for a lie. My whole life was based on a lie. I was twenty-eight years old, and the one I had lived for – Chairman Mao – was gone. He had been exposed as nothing more than a maniac, manipulating people who could be tricked in this way because they did not know the true God. We had followed a wicked man who wanted to eradicate all laws but his own, defining evil and good according to his own selfish ends. Somehow, we had not known any better.

(This is a fictionalized confession based on actual historic events and the true, first-hand accounts of several Chinese citizens who survived the Cultural Revolution).

FROM THE BIBLE:

But when the Pharisees heard that he had silenced the Sadducees, they gathered together. And one of them, a lawyer, asked him a question to test him. "Teacher, which is the great commandment in the Law?" And he said to him, "You shall love the Lord your God with all your heart and with all your soul and with all your mind. This is the great and first commandment. And a second is like it: You shall love your neighbor as yourself. On these two commandments depend all the Law and the Prophets." (Matthew 22:34-40)

TALKING IT OVER:

1. Look at the list of the commandments in catechism questions 83-94. Which of these were violated in the above story?

2. In what ways do you think your country respects or disrespects God's commands?

3. Why do you think Christians and churches are persecuted during times when God's law is rejected? Will you obey and defend God's commands regardless of the cost?

The Purpose of the Law

QUESTIONS TO LEARN:

95. Can any man keep these Ten Commandments perfectly?

No mere man, since the fall of Adam, ever did or can keep the Ten Commandments perfectly.

96. Of what use are the Ten Commandments to us?

They teach us our duty, and show us our need of a Savior.

*   *   *

Jesus' response to the rich young ruler's questions about eternal life highlights God's main purpose for the Ten Commandments – to reveal our hopeless unrighteousness and our need for Christ's atonement. Jonathan Edwards, who preached during America's eighteenth-century Great Awakening, understood this purpose well as he struggled to properly show God's moral perfection to an indifferent people desperately in need of redemption.

How to Get Through the Eye of a Needle

The sinking of the sun below the desert horizon might have reminded the young ruler of the very important question he had come to ask Jesus. Just as the sun had set and so ended the day, there would be a day when his life would set and he would be plunged into eternity. And on that day all his earthly riches would not ensure his eternal happiness. Perhaps Jesus could set his mind at rest on this matter?

As the rich young ruler entered the Judean town where he had heard that Jesus was teaching, he came upon a man surrounded by children near the town well. The man held the children close to Him and gently touched the heads of those on the edges of the circle. Even from a distance, the power of this man's touch was unmistakable.

Surprising himself as much as the servants that accompanied him, the rich young ruler ran to the man and fell on his knees before Him. "Good teacher," he said to Jesus, "what must I do to gain eternal life?"

"You know the commandments," Jesus answered. *"Do not murder, do not commit adultery, do not steal,* do not lie, honor your parents."

Any God-fearing Jew knew those laws, thought the ruler. And if anyone had kept them, he had. Why, who could claim that he had been dishonest in a single one of his many important dealings? Who could point to another man's possession that he had ever coveted or taken, or had any need of taking? If obedience to those laws was all that was required, surely he had already won eternal life!

"Teacher," he answered Jesus hopefully, *"All these I have kept since I was a boy."*

But Jesus looked back at him with doubt in His eyes. Was it doubt, or sadness? Why, it was pity!

"One thing you lack," Jesus said.

What could it be? The young ruler strained closer so he could hear His next words.

"Go, sell everything you have and give to the poor, and you will have treasure in heaven. Then come, follow me," Jesus said quite tenderly, considering the harshness of what He was suggesting.

Had the young ruler heard correctly? Jesus wanted him to give away his riches? "But if I do that, I will surely forfeit the happiness I now enjoy! No longer will I have important dealings to engage in. No longer will I have more than other men, or be able to do good to others." Faced with the costly invitation Jesus gave, the young man realized how attached he was to all his fine things and the influence they gave him over others. He could not let them go.

With obvious compassion, Jesus turned His eyes upon the young man.

"How hard it is for the rich to enter the kingdom of God! Indeed, it is easier for a camel to go through the eye

of a needle than for a rich man to enter the kingdom of God," He said to the ruler and to the surrounding crowd that had witnessed their exchange.

After a last, longing look at Jesus, the young ruler walked slowly away, his shoulders drooping. He had a picture in his mind of a camel refusing to cross a desert, much less being able and willing to go through the eye of a needle! And he wondered if all his lofty activities – his supposed generosity and honesty – amounted to nothing more than threading a single tail hair of a camel through a needle's eye!

Using the Ten Commandments, Jesus had gently shown the rich young ruler that he had failed to obey even the first of God's laws. He loved his riches more than he loved God! Thus, he fell short of the standard required to merit eternal life: a pure heart. In fact, all people fall short. For the rich young ruler, it was the pleasures of wealth that caused him to fall short; for others, it is the despair of poverty, bitterness, laziness, jealousy, fear of what people will think of them, or any number of the other selfish responses and desires of our fallen, sinful natures.

After the ruler had slipped sadly off, a concerned disciple asked Jesus, *"Who then can be saved?"*

"With man this is impossible, but not with God; all things are possible with God," Jesus answered. God alone can make us righteous. He does this through Christ paying the price for our sin (atonement), by giving (imputing) Christ's righteousness to those who repent and believe in Him, and by sending us His Holy Spirit who leads us to love

and want to please God more than we want to please ourselves.

(Taken from Matthew 19:16-30; Mark 10:17-30; Luke 18:18-30)

FROM THE BIBLE:

For whoever keeps the whole law but fails in one point has become accountable for all of it. (James 2:10)

So then, the law was our guardian until Christ came, in order that we might be justified by faith. (Galatians 3:24)

TALKING IT OVER:

1. *Did the rich young ruler keep the Ten Commandments? Why do you say this? Why did he think he had?*

2. *Why did Jesus tell the rich young ruler that he needed to give all he had to the poor in order to gain eternal life? (Jesus showed the young man his idolatry and covetousness, revealing that he did not deserve eternal life based on his own merit.)*

3. *Can we get to heaven by keeping the Ten Commandments? Then why did Jesus bring up the Ten Commandments in a conversation about eternal life?*

4. *Consider catechism questions 28-31. In our own nature, are we capable of keeping the commandments?*

Awakening Slumbering Saints

In 1733, the birds seemed to sing merrier songs in Northampton, Massachusetts, than they did most places. The yards were surely greener, the families bigger, the animals healthier, and the crops taller. Two hundred families bustled in the township's clean-lined and closely-built New England homes, and residents of even smaller hamlets all around Northampton came in to shop, socialize, and go to Sunday meeting. The church pastored by Jonathan Edwards boasted four to five hundred who regularly received the Lord's Supper.

In the eighty or so years since Northampton had first been settled, the church had only had three pastors. The second one was Edwards' grandfather, the beloved Solomon Stoddard, who had tended the flock in Northampton for sixty years before he died in 1729.

Edwards was honored to inherit this grandfather's post in one of the most important churches west of Boston. He hoped to experience some of the outpouring of God's Spirit that Mr. Stoddard had witnessed on occasion during the early days of Northampton. The last of these awakenings of the townspeople had been in 1718, fifteen years before. After that, everyone had settled down to living – adding to their families and following the ways of proper society, always careful to comply with the requirements of church membership. Yes, Jonathan Edwards could count on some of the most responsible church members in those parts.

But from his pulpit in the old church on Meetinghouse Hill, Edwards knew that things in Northampton were not as they seemed. He knew of the dutiful indifference with which many in his congregation received the Lord's Supper and attended church meetings. He knew that most of his flock no longer grasped God's majesty and holiness, as the community often had under Stoddard. They had grown cold to the sin that ruled them. Certainly they knew about God, but they did not fear Him in their hearts. Edwards saw that the people offered God nothing but ritual and habit.

Something else was also wrong in Northampton. It was in Edwards' own heart, and God had recently been powerfully convicting him of it. Edwards had never been so completely aware of his sin and inadequacies as he had been since he'd come to Northampton. Also, Edwards began to suspect that he had not preached a clear enough message to the people of Northampton. Had he offered them merely a bandage to fix a badly broken arm? Certainly he had often urged them to be righteous so that they could live pleasant, fruitful lives, assuring them that the unrighteousness that some of them persisted in would only leave them bitter and guilty. But in preaching this, had he contributed to their belief that they were able to be good and holy in themselves, and that this appearance of righteousness was all there was to being a Christian?

About this time, God sent His Holy Spirit among the youth of the Northampton church and led them to begin meeting together and praying for revival. God also gave Edwards a message through the writings of his wise old grandfather, who had warned young pastors: "It is a dismal thing to give men sleepy potions and make them sleep the sleep of death." Edwards realized he must do his part to awaken his congregation. He had to tell them the whole truth.

So, late in 1734, Jonathan Edwards began preaching a series of sermons explaining the Bible's teaching on the state of those who have not been justified by faith in Christ alone. In one sermon, on *The Justice of God in the Damnation of Sinners*, Edwards accused the people of boldly and habitually breaking God's laws and told them where this sin was *really* leading them – not just to difficulty in the present life, but to be cast out of heaven forever by a holy God. He preached:

Look over your past life … How deep have been the abominations of your life! … You have acted indecently on the Lord's day and in his house! … What a wicked attitude some of you have had towards your parents. Haven't you even harbored ill-will and malice toward them? What revenge and malice you have shown toward your neighbors! For the things of this world, you have envied and hated your neighbor; for the world you have thrown Christ and heaven behind your backs; for the

world you have sold your souls ... How much of a spirit of pride has appeared in you, the very spirit of the devil. You have shown off your appearance, your riches, your knowledge and abilities! ... What lies some of you have been guilty of, especially in your youth! How sensual you have been, and how intemperate. You have spent your precious time drinking at the tavern, or indulging yourselves day to day, and night to night, in all manner of evil imaginings ... God and your own consciences know what abominable things you have practiced when you have been alone ... And how you have corrupted others as well as polluting yourselves!

No one in the congregation could have any reason to mistakenly believe they were acceptable to God on the basis of their own merits. So, Edwards concluded, "Though it would be righteous in God forever to cast you off, and destroy you, yet it would also be just in God to save you, in and through Christ."[1]

Through Edwards' very clear sermons on the huge gulf between God's holiness and man's sin, God showed many in Northampton their desperate need for Christ. As the Holy Spirit led them more and more to see that their show of religion and ritual failed to meet God's holy standards, the people of Northampton and surrounding towns spiritually awoke to the fear of God. They knew that it would be completely just of God to

1. Patricia J. Tracy, *Jonathan Edwards, Pastor: Religion and Society in Eighteenth-Century Northampton* (New York: Hill and Wang, 1979), 83-84.

condemn them to hell. After first burdening them with this condemnation, the Holy Spirit eventually unburdened a great many through belief in a sufficient redeemer – Jesus Christ. These finally were awakened to a loving yet holy God. Now they genuinely desired to obey His commands.

FROM THE BIBLE:

Now we know that whatever the law says it speaks to those who are under the law, so that every mouth may be stopped, and the whole world may be held accountable to God. For by works of the law no human being will be justified in his sight, since through the law comes knowledge of sin. (Romans 3:19-20)

TALKING IT OVER:

1. *How do you think the Ten Commandments reveal God's own holiness? How did the people's new awareness of the Ten Commandments also help them to know God better?*

2. *Were the people of Northampton living up to God's standards of holiness?*

3. *What were the results of Edwards preaching the underlying principles of the Ten Commandments?*

BIBLIOGRAPHY

Unit 4 – Our Response to the Gospel
Spurgeon
Ernest W. Bacon, *Spurgeon: Heir of the Puritans* (London: George Allen & Unwin, 1967).

W.Y. Fullerton, *Charles Haddon Spurgeon, A Biography* (1920 ed.; Chicago: Moody Press, 1966).

Hugh T. Kerr and John M. Mulder, eds. *Famous Conversions, The Christian Experience* (Grand Rapids: Wm. B. Eerdmans Publishing Co., 1983).

Finney
Charles G. Finney, *The Memoirs of Rev. Charles G. Finney* (New York: A.S. Barnes & Co., [1876]).

Charles E. Hambrick-Stowe, *Charles G. Finney and the Spirit of American Evangelicalism* (Grand Rapids: Wm. B. Eerdmans Publishing Co., 1996).

John Williamson Nevin, "The Anxious Bench" in Keith J. Hardman, ed. *Issues in American Christianity: Primary Sources with Introductions* (Grand Rapids: Baker Books, 1993).

Mark A. Noll, *A History of Christianity in the United States and Canada* (Grand Rapids: Wm. B. Eerdmans Publishing Co., 1992).

J.I. Packer, *A Quest for Godliness, The Puritan Vision of the Christian Life* (Wheaton, IL: Crossway Books, 1990).

Maccabees
William Reuben Farmer, *Maccabees, Zealots, and Josephus: An Inquiry into Jewish Nationalism in the Greco-Roman Period* (New York: Columbia University Press, 1956).

Josephus, *Complete Works of Josephus In Ten Volumes.* Vol. 4. *Antiquities of the Jews Books X-XIII* (New York:

World Syndicate Publishing Co., 1900).

Sidney Tedesche, trans. *The First Book of Maccabees* 1.20-2.27 (New York: Harper & Brothers, 1950).

Judson

Courtney Anderson, *To the Golden Shore: The Life of Adoniram Judson* (Boston: Little, Brown and Co., 1956).

James D. Knowles, *Memoir of Mrs. Ann H. Judson* (1831 ed.; repr. New York: Garland Publishing, 1987).

Unit 5 – The Ten Commandments
Alfred the Great

Eleanor Shipley Duckett, *Alfred the Great* (Chicago: University of Chicago Press, 1956).

P.J. Helm, *Alfred the Great* (New York: Thomas Y. Crowell Co., 1963).

Boniface

Eleanor Shipley Duckett, *Anglo-Saxon Saints and Scholars* (New York: The Macmillan Co., 1947).

Kenneth Scott Latourette, *A History of Christianity. Volume I: To A.D. 1500* (Rev. ed.; Peabody, MA: Prince Press, 1997).

C.H. Talbot, trans./ed., *The Anglo-Saxon Missionaries in Germany* (New York: Sheed and Ward, 1954).

Jerome

J.N.D. Kelly, *Jerome: His Life, Writings, and Controversies* (London: Gerald Duckworth & Co., 1975).

Regine and Madeleine Pernoud, *Saint Jerome*, trans. Rosemary Sheed (New York: The MacMillan Co., 1962).

Eugene F. Rice Jr., *Saint Jerome in the Renaissance* (Baltimore and London: The Johns Hopkins University Press, 1985).

Jean Steinmann, *Saint Jerome and His Times*, trans. Ronald Matthews (Notre Dame, IN: Fides Publishers, n.d.).

Sunday School

Frank Booth, *Robert Raikes of Gloucester* (England: National Christian Education Council, Robert Denholm House, 1980).

Alfred Gregory, *Robert Raikes: Journalist and Philanthropist* (New York: Anson D.F. Randolph & Co., n.d.).

China's Cultural Revolution

Richard C. Bush Jr., *Religion in Communist China* (Nashville and New York: Abingdon Press, 1970).

Jung Chang, *White Swans, Three Daughters of China* (New York: Anchor Books, 1991).

Feng Jicai, *Ten Years of Madness, Oral Histories of China's Cultural Revolution* (San Francisco: China Books & Periodicals, 1996).

Donald E. MacInnis, *Religious Policy and Practice in Communist China* (New York: The Macmillan Co., 1972).

Ross Terrill, *The White-Boned Demon, A Biography of Madame Mao Zedong* (New York: William Morrow and Co., 1984).

Edwards

M.X. Lesser, *Jonathan Edwards* (Boston: Twayne Publishers, 1988).

Iain H. Murray, *Jonathan Edwards, A New Biography* (Edinburgh: The Banner of Truth Trust, 1987).

Patricia J. Tracy, *Jonathan Edwards, Pastor: Religion and Society in Eighteenth-Century Northampton* (New York: Hill and Wang, 1979).

Ola Elizabeth Winslow, *Jonathan Edwards* (New York: The Macmillan Co., 1940).

BUILDING ON THE ROCK SERIES
by Joel R. Beeke and Diana Kleyn

How God Used a Thunderstorm
ISBN: 978-1-85792-815-0

How God Stopped the Pirates
ISBN: 978-1-85792-816-7

How God Used a Snowdrift
ISBN: 978-1-85792-817-4

How God Used a Drought and an Umbrella
ISBN: 978-1-85792-818-1

How God Sent a Dog to Save a Family
ISBN: 978-1-85792-819-8

OTHER BOOKS IN THE
BIG BIBLE ANSWERS SERIES

THE STARRY MESSENGER

The evening of January 8th, 1610, was a clear and starry one in Padua, Italy, where Galileo Galilei taught mathematics at the leading university of that day. As Galileo studied the order and beauty he found through the telescope, he became one of the first to hypothesize that God holds his creation together in part through mathematical "laws" that keep the universe ticking like a well-designed clock. God's power and glory were clearly revealed in this precision instrument called the universe.

ISBN: 978-1-78191-863-0

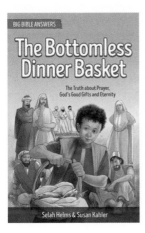

THE BOTTOMLESS
DINNER BASKET

The boy's father grabbed his hand and led him quickly down the path that would take them to the shore of the Sea of Galilee. Long before he saw Jesus, the boy heard the excited exclamations of the people around him. "There he is coming in that boat with his disciples!" someone cried, pointing dramatically out to sea.

ISBN: 978-1-78191-874-6

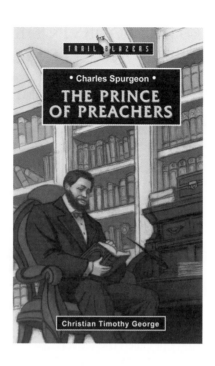

The Prince of Preachers: Charles Spurgeon
by Christian Timothy George

Charles Spurgeon was a simple country lad who went on to become one of the best known preachers in London, Europe and the world. Caught in a snowstorm one day when he was a teenager, he crept into the back of a church and the words "Look unto Jesus and be saved!" changed his whole life. Charles spoke words that touched the hearts of rich and poor alike. His fame became so widespread that it is reputed that even Queen Victoria went to hear one of his sermons. Charles was more concerned about the King of Kings – Jesus Christ.

ISBN: 978-1-78191-528-8

OTHER BOOKS IN THE
TRAILBLAZERS SERIES

TRAIL BLAZERS

• Jonathan Edwards •

AMERICA'S GENIUS

Christian Timothy George